How to draw like a fashion designer

Celia Joicey and Dennis Nothdruft

How to draw like a fashion designer

Celia Joicey and Dennis Nothdruft

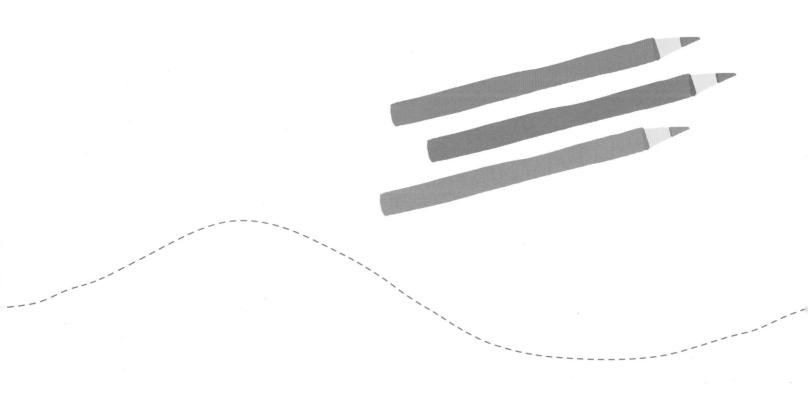

Thames & Hudson

Inspiration
06

Let's draw the basics
28

Let's design
80

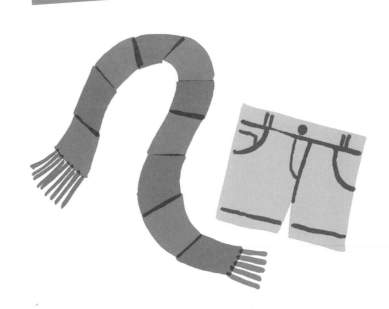

Hello, I'm Zandra Rhodes. I'm a fashion and textile designer. I hope that you'll find lots to inspire your fashion drawing on the pages that follow.

For a designer, drawing is a way of finding time to look and think. It is a **way of solving problems** – to take a photograph is too easy. It is important to **go out and observe** what's around you. By drawing you learn to see things from different perspectives. It is only when I draw that I am forced to understand the way that things are constructed.

I often find the **inspiration for my designs** when I draw. The process of drawing requires me to coordinate my eyes, hand and brain. What I see with my eyes and draw with my hand also gets filtered through my brain, so I can end up with ideas I would never have thought of otherwise.

Where I do my drawing plays a part too. I nearly always get inspired when I am travelling. My rule when I travel and am away from my studio is to **do a drawing a day**. It need not be a textile or an idea for a dress – it could be an animal. But it has to be a drawing, and one that might just lead to a new design. It is wonderful to look back on a trip and see that you have managed to do a drawing every day.

I began to be sure that I wanted to be a designer when I first went to art college. At first, drawing led me to think of a career in book illustration. But I soon learned that **drawing is a foundation for all design** and I naturally drifted into being a textile designer, which I really enjoy. I love the way **textiles influence the shape of a garment**, and how the print can achieve wonderful things.

I suppose I have always drawn and painted to gain inspiration. Indeed, one of my reasons for establishing the Fashion and Textile Museum in London is my belief in how seeing and drawing the exhibits in museums can stimulate ideas.

Drawing is my foundation for **seeing and thinking in original ways**. I hope this book will demonstrate the key role that drawing can play and will give confidence to all young artists setting out on a career in design.

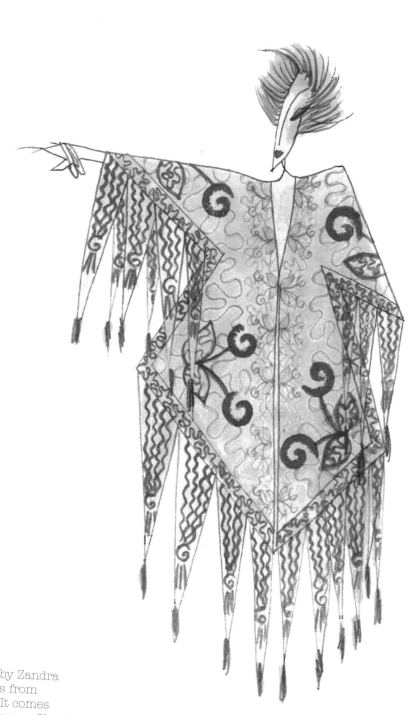

This design by Zandra Rhodes dates from about 1970. It comes from her Chevron Shawl Collection, and features her characteristic 'magic head' figure.

So you want to draw like a designer?

This book shows you how to follow the same step-by-step process that you would use in workshops at the Fashion and Textile Museum in London. It is divided into three sections: *Inspiration*, *Let's draw the basics* and *Let's design*.

Anna Sui sketches in pencil then uses coloured markers to show the detail of lace and ruffles.

Inspiration

The first section of this book is all about inspiring you to design great clothes. It includes interviews with some of the most famous fashion designers in the world, and shows some of their drawings.

Study the drawings and read the interviews to discover how these designers developed their own drawing styles, and learn all kinds of techniques, tips and tricks.

Take inspiration from these designers, but remember: it's just as important to develop your own individual drawing style that shows your ideas in a way that is special to you. Remember to keep your sketches too so that you can refer back to them.

Zandra Rhodes is known for the gorgeous colours and rich patterns of the textiles she uses.

Bellville Sassoon evening gowns create a mood of elegance and sophisticated glamour.

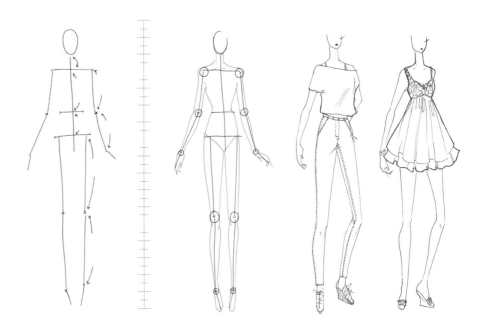

Let's draw the basics

Before you can begin designing, you need to learn the basics of drawing. This section starts by showing you how to draw a 'croquis', or figure shape. Once you can draw your croquis with confidence, you can begin designing your clothes around it – from dresses, skirts and shirts through to trousers, jackets, coats and party wear.

In this section, you'll also find drawing tips and suggestions for how you can vary your designs, as well as places to look for more inspiration.

Let's draw the basics guides you through all the stages you will need, from drawing your basic figure to designing clothes to dress your figure.

Let's design

You've looked at the work of famous designers, you've learnt how to draw a croquis and different types of garment – now it's time to start designing. This section explains how to get started by doing research, developing your ideas and sorting through them so that you can build your own fashion collection.

It also explains the kind of training you might need to get into the fashion industry, and describes the different jobs you can do.

At the end of the book, there's a list explaining what particular words mean, and an index so you can easily find what you are looking for inside the book.

You'll need a variety of materials for your designer's kit. You'll need to do research too. The *Let's Design* chapter tells you how.

"I draw anywhere I can."

Name
Zandra Rhodes
Born
1940, Chatham, Kent, UK
Design training
Medway College of Art, Kent, and Royal College of Art, London
Trademark style
Theatrical, glamorous and extrovert

Background

Zandra Rhodes is a British designer who helped London to become a leading centre of international fashion in the 1970s. At art college, she specialized in printed textiles. Since then, she has played an important role in making printed patterns fashionable.

Her pink hair and colourful make-up are part of Zandra Rhodes' look but she uses these elements in her drawings too. Her clients range from rock stars to royalty, and her vintage designs are popular with celebrities including Kate Moss, Kelly Osbourne and Ashley Olsen. In 1977, she launched her pink and black jersey collection, which she called 'Conceptual Chic'. The designs had holes in them and beaded safety pins, and earned her the name 'Princess of Punk'.

Zandra Rhodes has also designed sets and costumes for the opera.

Over 500 illustrations can be accessed from the Zandra Rhodes Digital Study Collection *www.zandrarhodes. ucreative.ac.uk*.

Interview

What inspires you to draw?
Time and space are important. But if something catches my eye I must draw it there and then, even if it is 4 o'clock in the morning.

Where do you draw?
I draw mainly in my sketchbook because I lose everything! But if the drawing is in a sketchbook my ideas are safe. I start at page one and use all the pages until I get to the back. I draw anywhere I can.

What media do you like best?
Japanese felt-tip pens on Japanese rice paper.

How do you start your design drawings?
I drape the printed textile in different ways on my body or on the stand and try to think about how it would look made up. Then I draw what's in front of me.

Do your drawings always look like the finished garment?
No, but the drawing provides inspiration throughout the design process.

How does a drawing become a finished garment?
There are lots of stages. Initially, my drawings are given to the pattern cutter.

Do you keep your drawings?
Yes, in my sketchbooks.

Do you have a favourite drawing?
No I don't. I am fortunate that the University for the Creative Arts (UCA) has digitized my archive so it is now even easier for me to access and refer to previous work.

The Conceptual Chic Collection includes clothes with holes made and stitched to look like tears. These tears are caught with beaded safety pins and chains. The dresses have their seams on the outside.

Zandra Rhodes designed her Mexico Collection in 1976. The print was inspired by a type of Mexican hat called a sombrero. It is full of wonderful colours and textile patterns. It shows how a designer can take inspiration from all sorts of different places.

Name
Valentino

Born
1932, Voghera, Italy

Design training
École des Beaux-Arts, Paris, and Chambre Syndicale de la Couture Parisienne. Worked initially with Jacques Fath, Balenciaga, Jean Dessès and Guy Laroche

Trademark style
Opulent, ultra-feminine designs for Hollywood icons in 'Valentino Red' – his signature colour

"I remember with love my first drawings."

Background

Valentino Garavani, often known simply as Valentino, is a fashion designer and master couturier. He founded his fashion house in Rome in the late 1950s and since then has been designing for the world's most glamorous women.

From the time he began in the industry, Valentino and long-time partner Giancarlo Giammetti have built the Valentino brand into one of the most famous names in international fashion.

Sophistication, stylishness and luxury are all part of Valentino's signature style. Chiffons, silks, satins and delicate laces are among the fabrics he uses to flatter women's figures and make them look more feminine. His work is also known for its exquisite detailing and embroidery.

Valentino retired from his career in fashion in 2008.

To learn more about him, visit *www.valentinogaravanimuseum.com*. There are more than 150 original drawings on the site, as well as 5,000 pictures that record his career.

Interview

What inspires you to draw?
The responsibility to deliver the work to hundreds of people.

Where do you draw?
Mostly in my office.

What medium do you like best?
Pencil.

How do you start your design drawings?
From the head, the hair and mostly by profile. A long neck has more style.

Do your drawings always look like the finished garment?
Yes, I very rarely change during fittings, a detail maybe, but the silhouette stays.

How does a drawing become a finished garment?
It is a long process; choice of fabric as first step, the cutting, the fittings, choice of buttons. There is a lot of attention, work and people involved.

How important is drawing to your business today?
Everything I do, even a costume for a ballet or a sofa for my house, needs an explanation and I do it by sketching.

Do you keep your drawings?
Of course, thousands of them.

Are there any drawings that are really special to you?
No, there are too many. I do remember with love my first drawings when I was working in Paris.

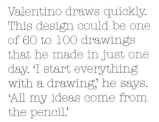

Valentino draws quickly. This design could be one of 60 to 100 drawings that he made in just one day. 'I start everything with a drawing,' he says. 'All my ideas come from the pencil.'

The slim pencil skirt of this daytime outfit contrasts beautifully with the wide sleeves, wide stand-up collar and full outline of the swing jacket. Drawing the figure in side view shows off the shapes really clearly.

Using just a few lines, Valentino is able to create a mood and give essential information about a design. This simple outline shows a short cocktail dress. The most detailed part is the gathered area, with buttons, at the waist.

For evening glamour, Valentino designed this long dress with a draped and fitted bodice and a layered flared skirt.

Name
David Sassoon

Born
1932, London

Design training
Hammersmith School of Art and Royal College of Art, London

Trademark style
High-society glamour; elegant wedding dresses and romantic evening wear

"New fabrics can inspire a drawing."

Background

Bellville Sassoon is one of Britain's best-known couture labels. It was founded by designer Belinda Bellville in 1953. In 1958, David Sassoon joined the company.

In the 1960s, Bellville Sassoon began to design clothes for fashionable weddings and balls. Some of the world's most stylish women have worn their dresses. The label was a favourite of royal clients, such as Princess Margaret, Princess Anne, Princess Michael of Kent and Diana, Princess of Wales.

As the company got bigger, a team of designers helped David Sassoon to develop his ideas further. These include Shena Carslaw, Helen Storey, George Sharp and Romy Gelardin.

In the 1980s Bellville Sassoon, with designer Lorcan Mullany, expanded the ready-to-wear collections and more people could afford their clothes. The company also continues to create dressmaking patterns for Vogue Patterns. Anyone who can sew can buy one of these patterns and make their own designer clothes themselves.

Interview

What inspires you to draw?
Sometimes new fabrics can inspire a drawing but it can be anything, from a mood to a book, a film, or the fantasy they inspire.

Where do you draw?
Usually at home. When I was at college I always drew out my ideas or roughs at home. At Bellville Sassoon, I drew the roughs at home then I would refine each drawing in the studio whilst an assistant pinned the design in toile, which is a fabric used to test out the design. As the company grew, I passed my initial rough sketches to one of the team to create more drawings – up to 20 for each design.

What medium do you like best?
For rough drawings, I like to use a thick pen for effects and different textures.

How do you start your design drawings?
I start with the body. I rarely draw the head – it is a question of time. To speed up the design process, I might draw over a pattern of a body too.

Do your drawings always look like the finished garment?
Mostly they do. You can exaggerate fashion in the initial rough but by the final drawing, the design has been reworked to take account of the toile and fabric choices. On the whole this final drawing doesn't change.

How does a drawing become a finished garment?
It can take up to six months but the drawing provides the inspiration.

Do you keep your drawings?
Yes. I have some of my student sketches. The rest can be seen in the archives of the Fashion Museum in Bath [in the west of England].

Are there any drawings that are really special to you?
I have quite a few. The earliest is one I made at the Royal College of Art. It was a technically difficult design but I made the dress successfully so this has happy memories.

'La Goulue' is a slender black slip swept with a flurry of white flamenco ruffles, from 1968.

David Sassoon's favourite sketch is this rose print organza dress. It was part of his Royal College of Art final year show in 1958.

This specially commissioned, hand-embroidered, gold-beaded couture dress was made for the singer Madonna. The felt-pen drawing by George Sharp dates from 1999.

Name
Peter Jensen
Born
1969, Løgstør, Denmark
Design training
The Royal Danish Academy of Fine Arts, School of Design, Copenhagen, and Central Saint Martins, London. Also trained in graphic design, embroidery and tailoring before studying fashion
Trademark style
Cool and clever basics for men and women

Peter Jensen having a good laugh, in a favourite photo.

Background

Peter Jensen is known for his youthful and fun fashion designs. His womenswear collections are often inspired by a real woman whose style and attitude he likes. Among the famous women who have inspired him are the American photographer Cindy Sherman, the American movie star Sissy Spacek and the British sculptor Barbara Hepworth.

In 1999, Jensen graduated from Central Saint Martins and launched his menswear label. He introduced womenswear soon afterwards. His designs are sold in major stores and boutiques around the world, from New York to Tokyo. He has also worked with international retail chains, such as Topshop, Topman and Urban Outfitters.

In 2009, the Danish Arts Council gave Peter Jensen an important award. Normally this prize is given only to fine artists. Since then his designs have been displayed in the Copenhagen Arts Museum and the Victoria and Albert Museum in London.

Interview

What inspires you to draw?
It is all to do with things going on in my head and getting them out so I can communicate what the collection is about with my team. I have a routine when I start the new season. I always watch a Danish television series from the 1970s which is about different groups of people in Denmark from 1929 to 1946. It lets me focus on what I do, without any guilt or pressure.

Where do you draw?
At home in front of the television or in a hotel.

What media do you like best?
Pen and paper, nothing else.

How do you start your design drawings?
With the head.

Do your drawings always look like the finished garment?
More or less. I was trained at Saint Martins which makes you look, look, look at your drawings before you start any 3D work.

How does a drawing become a finished garment?
By doing a lot of fitting on a perfect body.

How important is drawing to your business today?
It is key, no question about it. Otherwise I don't have a tool to talk about. Does that make sense?

Do you keep your drawings?
Yes, I have most of them from way back.

Do you have a favourite drawing?
No, the collection I'm working on always becomes the favourite.

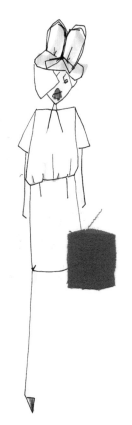

Peter Jensen's 'Thelma' collection was inspired by Thelma Speirs. She is a London milliner and one-half of the design team Bernstock Speirs.

It can be fun to design for a specific occasion. This dress design was worn by American filmmaker and actress Lena Dunham to the Grammy Awards ceremony in New York.

xFacing inside
x Lined

net

This design for the 'Nina' collection, was inspired by singer, songwriter and pianist Nina Simone. It uses swatches of fabric to show the texture of the clothes.

Name
Christian Lacroix

Born
1951, Arles, France

Design training
University of Montpellier, the Sorbonne and École du Louvre, Paris

Trademark style
Fairytale dresses, rich colour and his signature puffball skirts

"More and more I draw on my computer graphic palette."

Background

Christian Lacroix is a French designer who has helped to revive the art of couture in Paris since the 1980s.

Lacroix was brought up in Arles where he developed his interest in historical costume. He studied art history and moved to Paris with the hope of becoming a museum curator. But after he was introduced to Karl Lagerfeld and other designers he began working for Hermès, and later for the house of Patou.

When Lacroix won the important Golden Thimble award in 1986, he was given support to set up his own fashion house. The haute-couture designs he created under his own name dazzled everyone in the world of fashion.

Over the past twenty years, Lacroix has also produced ready-to-wear fashion, perfume, jeans, childrenswear, lingerie, homeware and menswear couture. From 2002 to 2005 he worked for the Italian fashion house Pucci. Today he is best known for his designs for the theatre, opera and ballet.

Interview

What inspires you to draw?
Everything, anything, sometimes nothing.

Where do you draw?
Anywhere, but more and more I draw on my computer graphic palette. Using this computer program has freed me from my fear of the blank page.

What media do you like best?
When I'm not using my computer, I like a simple ballpoint or felt pen and from time to time classic watercolour with gouache.

How do you start your drawings?
Usually I start with the head contours or even just an eye. I let go, following inspiration and the line, like a kind of automatic writing, sometimes with just a colour stain.

Do your drawings always look like the finished garment?
I love it when the girl in the final garment looks exactly like my first sketch. But a drawing can lead to a very different result. I remember a bathing suit that step by step was transformed into a wedding gown.

Do you keep your drawings?
I have kept as many as I can since my birth! I even have my kindergarten drawings and my scribbles. I should like to give everything to the museum in Arles.

Do you have a favourite drawing?
It depends on the day, the mood or the time. I rarely frame my sketches but there are four or five I have preserved.

The bright orange, red and pink colours in this drawing are typical of Lacroix, who is inspired by the warm colours of his childhood in the south of France.

When Lacroix designs, he first of all produces rough, fast sketches. 'These often turn out to be the best ideas on which I base all others,' he says.

Christian Lacroix is known for his dramatic fashion drawings in a variety of media. These examples have been drawn using digital techniques which are great for quick and immediate results.

"My interest in fashion began with a box of crayons."

Name
Norman Hartnell
Born
1901, London
Died
1979
Design training
Self-taught. He studied at Mill Hill School and Cambridge University, where he designed costumes for dramatic performances
Trademark style
Sophisticated glamour for royal and society women

Background

Norman Hartnell was England's best-known 20th-century couturier. He became famous for his elegant evening gowns and wedding dresses, and for the imaginative way he used satin, tulle, embroidery and trimmings. For inspiration, he liked to pin lengths of gold tissue to his curtains to see how the fabric would fall. He would also throw coloured satin across his sofa cushions and imagine that the cushions were bust and hips.

His designs were elaborate and he drew beautifully, but he relied on a workforce of around 550 people to help interpret his ideas. A large group of specialists sewed the embroidery on his gowns.

In 1938 Hartnell became official dressmaker to the British Royal Family. He created a fashion look for both the British Queen Mother and the present queen, Elizabeth II. When Elizabeth married in 1947, she wore a Hartnell wedding dress that was embroidered with 10,000 seed pearls and thousands of crystal beads. She also wore a Hartnell gown to her coronation in 1953.

Interview

Norman Hartnell died in 1979, so these extracts are taken from *Silver and Gold, The Autobiography of Norman Hartnell* (1955)

Where do you get your inspiration?
The dresses in the pictures of the great painters are often in my mind...

Where do you draw?
My house in Windsor Forest.

What media do you like best?
Sharp pencil, watercolour paints, sable-haired paintbrush. My interest in fashion began with a box of crayons. All of my school books on mathematics, geometry and algebra were covered with doodled designs of dresses.

How do you start your design drawings?
I sketch firstly the head, then roughly the limbs, turning the body towards its right, so that the left hip is foremost... Then the arms, one akimbo and one outstretched, to allow for the arrangement of the sleeves. Finally I draw the feet.

Is it easy to turn a drawing into a real, finished garment?
[Hartnell worked with Miss Doherty and Madame Germaine Davide, a French fitter, to realise his elaborate sketches.] Helped by these two meticulous women, who judged the value of my sketches and advised on style and cut respectively, my work took on a new aspect. I was beginning to understand how much lay between the designing of a dress and its transformation into something that women would buy.

How does a drawing become a finished garment?
On returning to my business house I discuss all these designs with my tailors and head vendeuses. After a few days we begin the fittings. The last rite, before showing to the Press, the buyers and the public, is the dress rehearsal.

Hartnell designed this full-skirted dress for Queen Elizabeth II in the 1940s. It was a look that he created for the Queen and her mother. He was inspired by portraits he saw in Buckingham Palace of Victorian ladies in crinoline dresses.

This was the first cocktail dress created for Queen Elizabeth II when she was still a princess. Notice how long gloves complete all the outfits shown on this page.

Hartnell created this slim, gold dress for Queen Elizabeth to wear to a State Opening of Parliament. This is the annual event when a new British parliamentary session begins. Can you see the official robe she will wear in the background?

Name
Anna Sui
Born
1964, Detroit
Design training
Parsons School of Design,
New York
Trademark style
High-fashion runway mixed
with retro and rock 'n' roll

"I dress the girls up like paper dolls."

Background

Anna Sui is an American fashion designer whose collections include a treasure chest of retro looks. She is inspired by all kinds of themes, including rock and punk music and the Wild West.

Anna Sui studied design briefly but left art school to work in the fashion industry. Her lucky break happened when a buyer from the department store Macy's in New York spotted her collection of six pieces at a trade fair. Later, the collection was displayed in the Christmas window of the store.

For more than 10 years, Anna Sui ran her business from her apartment. Today she runs a worldwide fashion business, including ranges of clothing, shoes, eyewear and perfume.

Interview

How do you set about drawing?
I do quick pencil sketches to work out the details – the shape, seams, pockets, buttons – on specific garments. I do more finished sketches when I'm trying to plan how the collection will be worn on the catwalk.

Where do you draw?
At my desk in my office.

What do you like to draw with?
Coloured markers.

How do you start your design drawings?
I never trace the figures. They look like I do because they all have similar faces and poses, but I draw all the girls freehand and dress them up like paper dolls.

Do your drawings always look like the finished garment?
Remarkably so. I'm proud of how accurately I can draw printed fabrics and woven textures.

How does a drawing become a finished garment?
My quick sketches are given to our pattern makers to follow.

How important is drawing to your business today?
I think anything you can do to communicate your ideas clearly is a big help.

Do you keep your drawings?
Yes.

Are there any drawings that are really special to you?
I'm fond of the drawings I did for my Spring 2007 Rococo Pirate collection.

Anna's signature style includes rosy apple cheeks, red lipstick and a button eye. The heads of her figures are often cut off because she always draws right to the top of the page.

Coloured markers are a good way to show prints.

Notice how the colour palette works across this collection. A palette is the set of colours that a designer chooses to work with.

21st-century drawing

Do you use computers? They are essential to today's fashion industry. Many designers now use computer-aided design (CAD) programs – but the basics of drawing remain the same.

The designers on these two pages began working in the 21st century. They have trained with computers since school, but both know the importance of more traditional drawing tools.

'I draw from observation when I'm out and about, then in my studio.'

'I try to keep a lot of my drawings, even "failures": looking at them over and over helps you to pick out the formal issues and resolve them.'

Name
Kitty Joseph

British-born Kitty Joseph graduated from the Royal College of Art in London in 2011. She has become well-known for her figure-hugging 'bodycon' dresses, her jackets made from a stretchy rubber material called neoprene and her perspex accessories. She has created one-off pieces for Lady Gaga and has worked for brands such as Stylus and Nokia, as well as creating printed fabric designs for DKNY and Marks & Spencer.

"My drawings often begin with marks of colour."

Interview

What inspires you?
As a trained textile designer, I find my drawings often begin with marks of colour. These suggest garment shapes, which act as a canvas for my print designs.

How do you start work?
My initial drawings are quite free, focused on feeling and mood. I then have to technically pin things down - where is the line of that neckline or hem of a skirt. I like to work on top of my own templates, collaging pieces of paper and colour.

What is your favourite medium?
I like the challenge of using whatever's around when I feel the urge - I love scrawling with cheap biros. However I am most at home with my inks and Sennelier pastels because you can record colour so well with them.

How important is drawing to you?
Drawing is a language. Without it I don't think I would have developed my style to such a degree.

Do you like to draw on a computer?
While my training has taught me to value and use freely the tools of computer-aided design and other technologies, I prefer a direct process of design, working by hand with the human form.

'My favourite drawing is the first drawing I made of my signature 5-hooded hoody. I was inspired at the time and the drawings just flowed from my pen so naturally and effortlessly.'

Name
Alexandra Groover

This young designer trained at Rhode Island School of Design in the United States and at Central Saint Martins in London. She launched her own fashion label in London in 2008. She works with jersey fabric, moulding the fabric into bold shapes, almost like a sculpture. She also works with musicians, photographers and other designers on special projects.

"Every idea I have starts with a drawing."

Interview

What inspires you?
Everything in my life.

How do you start work?
I start with a theme for each season, while at the same time sketching different ideas that come to me. When the time comes to start completing the designs, I try to tie all of my ideas together to form a collection around the theme.

What is your favourite medium?
Mechanical pencil or black ballpoint pen. I try to keep a small sketchbook in my bag, but inspiration seems always to strike wherever I am, so I also have endless file folders of drawings on napkins, envelopes, receipts and business cards. When I have an idea, it doesn't matter where I am: I use whatever is available and always try to sketch it out before I forget it.

How important is drawing to you?
Every idea I have starts with a drawing. Sometimes at first they may be simple sketches that are not much to look at, but they always help me in visualizing my ideas.

Do you draw on a computer?
Draping fabric on a stand is definitely my favourite way of working. There are no rules for my approach but I usually start with a sketch of a garment or a geometric shape as a pattern, and then it begins to develop as I work with the fabric on the stand. Sometimes the garment looks like my sketch, and sometimes it changes into something completely different.

Old drawings can be useful. Both designers return to drawings to pick up unused ideas and details and translate them into new designs for a future season.

Why sketch?

The designers in this book believe that drawing is a way of thinking. It allows them to explore ideas. But it is also a way of remembering ideas. Sketchbooks are a helpful way of keeping your thoughts in one place. Many designers return to their earlier sketches to find new inspiration.

How many sketchbooks do designers use?

Some designers keep different sketchbooks for different things, such as drawings, cuttings and fabric swatches. Others keep everything in one book and work steadily through it page by page. Recording lots of different things side by side can spark ideas for a new design.

What sorts of sketchbooks do designers use?

Sketchbooks come in all shapes and sizes so it's a matter of personal choice. Some designers, such as Zandra Rhodes, like to keep a sketchbook on hand so they draw wherever they are. They need sketchbooks that are easy to carry.

There are different kinds of paper, too. It's important to choose the right kind to suit the drawing or painting materials you are using. For example, watercolour is a very wet paint and can make ordinary paper buckle. Think about the binding of the sketchbook too. Some are spiral-bound or glued on one edge, which can make it easier to tear out a finished drawing for reference later.

Drawing the real objects that you see around you sometimes leads to new ideas. This drawing of flowers by Zandra Rhodes could suggest a new shape or palette.

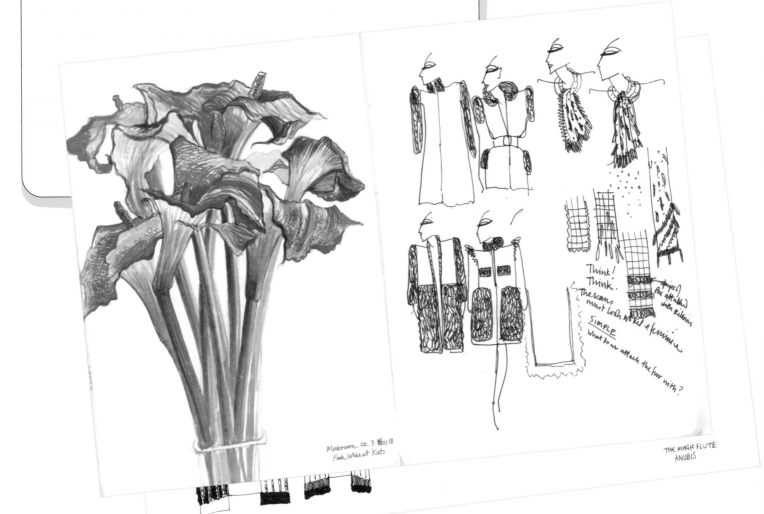

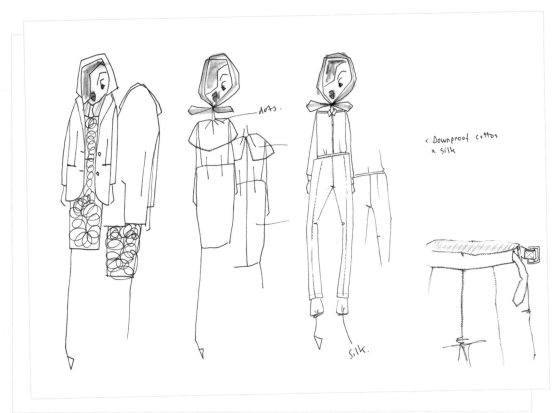

These drawings by Peter Jensen show how he uses his sketchbook to work out his designs. He highlights details and thinks about how each garment should be constructed.

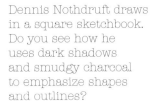

Dennis Nothdruft draws in a square sketchbook. Do you see how he uses dark shadows and smudgy charcoal to emphasize shapes and outlines?

Some designers use digital sketchbooks, or tablets, to record ideas quickly. These drawings by Christian Lacroix feature colour, which is much easier to add with a computer.

Getting prepared

The designers in this book use a range of different tools to draw with. Experiment to find out what suits you and your style best.

Here are the materials you will need to get together before you start drawing. Keep them together in a special box or place so you always have them ready.

Pencils

If you are designing, a hard pencil will help you to get a crisp line. The examples in this book were drawn with an HB pencil.

- For sketching or shading you should try **a softer pencil** such as 4B.
- Smaller items need to be drawn with care. Use **a hard pencil** to create a fine line to help highlight specific details.

H = hard   B = soft

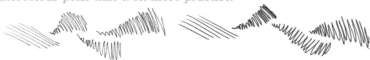

Pens

These are great for detail. There are lots of types to choose from, with tips of all sizes and widths.

- **Design markers** and **fineliners** are good to start with.
- If you plan to use paint alongside a design in ink, make sure you choose **waterproof pens** so that the colours don't run.
- Watercolour pens take a bit more practice.

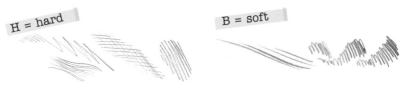

Gouache

Gouache paint is **opaque**, which means that you cannot see through it. It creates ares of solid colour, with neat, crisp edges.

- Make sure you **mix enough** of the same colour or you may not be able to match it exactly if you run out.
- Use lots of water to apply the paint smoothly and let each colour dry completely before you move onto the next one.
- For a **nice, clean edge**, outline each area of colour before filling it in.

Watercolour

This comes in tubes or pans and is slightly **transparent**, or see-through.

- Watercolour is great for working quickly and adding large areas, or **washes**, of colour.
- Because it is transparent, you cannot paint light colours over dark ones.

Brushes

Brushes are made of various different materials and the tips come in lots of different shapes and widths. If you are colouring your designs, use a **firm, fine brush** to give you a precise line.

Paper

Use a **thin, fine paper** so that you can overlay this on your croquis, or basic figure, and see the shape underneath.

- Remember that watercolour paper may pucker when you apply a wash.

Sketchbook

- Choose a sketchbook that you can carry around easily – **A4 or smaller** should be fine.
- Some sketchbooks include a **pocket**, which you can use to carry magazine cuttings, colour swatches, etc.

No rubbers, no rulers

The problem with a rubber is that it can stop you from **learning from your mistakes**. If a design isn't working, you won't find out why by removing the problem. Instead you should draw over it, and find a new line in a different direction. Avoid rulers too – they create hard, mechanical-looking lines.

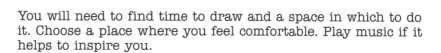

You will need to find time to draw and a space in which to do it. Choose a place where you feel comfortable. Play music if it helps to inspire you.

Where to work
Experiment with different positions for drawing. Working flat – on a table or at a desk, or even on the floor – may be right for you. Or perhaps you could try working on a board at an angle.

Why tracing is useful
Once you have drawn a croquis, or basic figure, that you are happy with, you can design quickly by drawing over the top of it. You can read more about this on page 37.
- Place a thin piece of paper over the croquis. Focus on drawing the clothing first. Think about how it sits on the figure.
- When you have completed your design, draw the head, arms, legs and feet, using the croquis as your guide.

The right line
A solid line indicates a seam and a broken line indicates decorative or top-stitching.

Adding shadows and depth
Small, crisscrossing marks – known as **crosshatching** – help to show areas of light and shade in a design. For example, in gathered fabric shadow shows where the fabric folds.

Which way round?
Drawing paper is usually rectangular in shape. You can place the paper so it forms an upright rectangle, known as **portrait** shape, or format; or you can turn it on its side so it forms a long rectangle, known as **landscape** format.
- To begin with, it helps to work in portrait format so that you have plenty of height for your croquis and design.
- When you are developing a collection, it can be more useful to work in landscape format so you can see your designs alongside each other and compare them.

portrait

landscape

Trying different media

Look at the drawings on these two pages. They all show the same figure but have been drawn with different media, from pencil and pen to paint. Can you see how changing the medium you use changes the look and feel of the drawing?

Try out different media to discover your favourites – those you feel most comfortable using, and that express your ideas best. Try combining different media, too.

Look back at the drawings by all the designers on the previous pages. Do you see how very different their styles are? What media have they used?

Which of their styles do you like best? Perhaps you could experiment by using some of their varied techniques to help you develop a signature style of your own.

1

2

Hard pencil

This creates a fine line that will highlight the structure and outline of your design. Use a hard pencil when you start drawing to help you focus on shape, outline and the details of how the garment is put together.

Soft pencil

Use a 4B or softer pencil to create a thick, dark line. Build up your drawing with shading and techniques such as crosshatching – lots of little crisscrossing lines – to add texture and 3D shape.

③

④

⑤

Pen

This versatile medium is good both for outlining and doing detailed drawing. Pens are a great way to give a confident look to your work.

India ink

Applied with a brush, India ink gives a soft line. You can use it diluted to fill in areas too. It's harder to control than other media but work with your 'mistakes' and follow where they take you.

Gouache and pen

At some point, you'll need to think about colour for your designs. When using gouache paint, apply it thickly for solid colour, or thinned-down for a wash. Don't worry if you go over the outlines – it will give your drawing extra character.

Step by step

When you're learning to do fashion drawing, a good tip is to break down your sketches into steps. Look at this croquis, or basic figure, that has been broken down into eight steps. On the following pages, follow each step closely and you'll be able to draw a croquis just like this one.

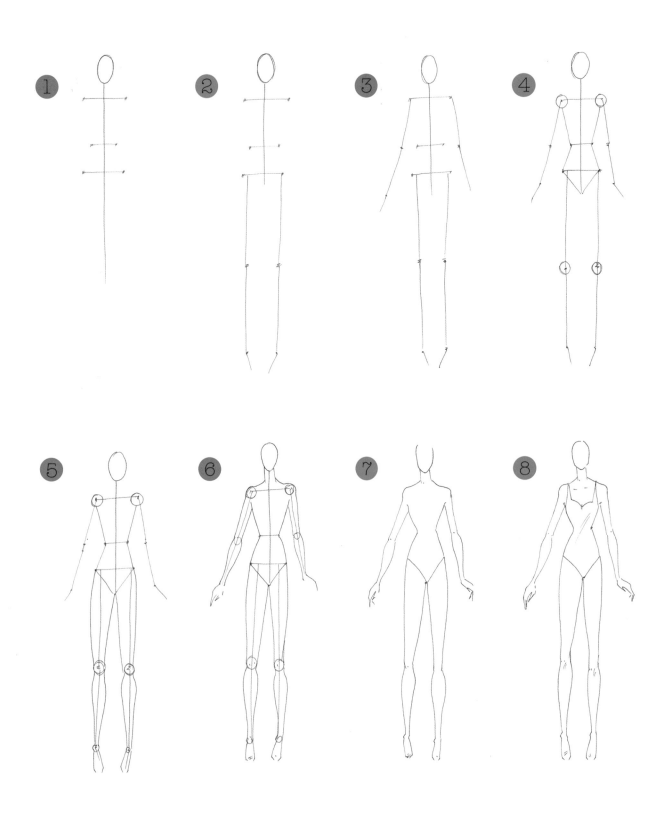

Body proportions

Did you know that most people are about seven-and-a-half heads tall? In fashion drawing, figures are usually taller than this – more than nine heads from head to foot. Remember this when you're drawing a croquis. It will help to keep your drawing in proportion.

Look at the measurements on this drawing. Is the distance from your shoulder to your elbow roughly one-and-a-half heads? Try comparing other measurements, too.

Joints and body markers

The shoulders, waist, hips and knees are joints that connect different parts of the body. They make helpful markers for a fashion designer. When you position these joints the correct distance apart, your croquis looks in proportion. Look at the labels for other parts of the body. These are also helpful to use as markers when you're drawing a croquis.

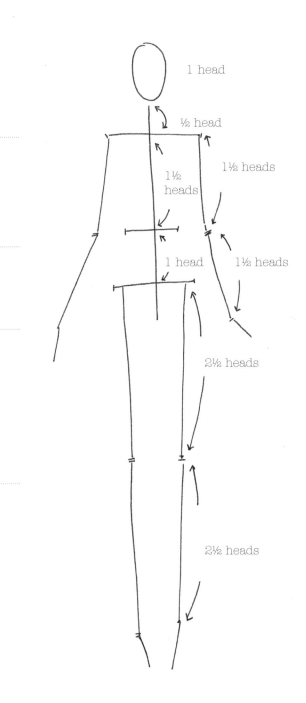

1 head
½ head
1½ heads
1½ heads
1 head
1½ heads
2½ heads
2½ heads

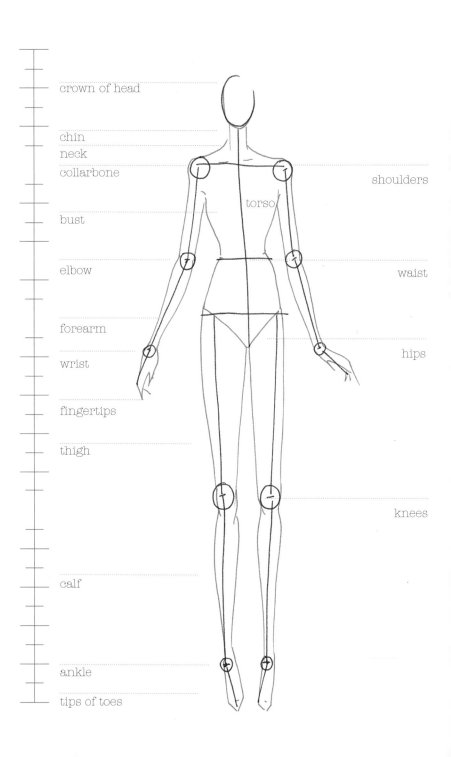

crown of head
chin
neck
collarbone
bust
elbow
forearm
wrist
fingertips
thigh
calf
ankle
tips of toes

shoulders
torso
waist
hips
knees

Head and spine

Draw the head. Imagine it's a grape.

Draw a line down from the head. This is the spine, or axis, on which to hang the rest of the body.

Add three lines for the shoulders, waist and hips. The neck is at least half the height of the head. The shoulders are the widest of the three lines.

To find the waist, measure the same height from the crown of the head to the shoulder line. The waist is about half the width of the shoulders.

Measure one head below the waist to find the hips. The hips are wider than the waist.

IDEA

To check that your drawing is in proportion, measure the height of the head on the page. Place the top of the pencil at the crown of the head and your thumb at the chin. Now make sure that everything is in correct proportion to the head height.

Legs

Put your pencil just inside the edge of the hips and drop down two lines for the legs.

Measure two-and-a-half heads below each hip to mark the knee.

Measure the same distance below each knee to mark the ankles.

Draw short lines for the feet.

IDEA

Practise keeping your pencil on the page to create a smooth line, not a jagged one.

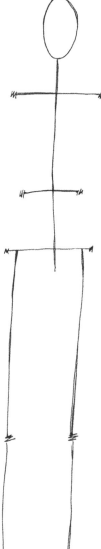

shoulders

waist

hips

knees

Arms

From the shoulder point, draw a smooth line as far as the waist and make a mark. This is the elbow. Match this on the other side.

To create each forearm, measure the same distance again with a smooth line from the elbow.

Make a mark for each wrist.

Add short lines for hands.

IDEA

Arms may be longer than you at first think. Check out their proportions by looking at your friends and family.

Shoulders, knees and torso

Draw two circles for the shoulders – imagine each one as a tennis ball. Create a similar shape for each knee.

Starting from each shoulder, draw a line to the waist. From the waist drop a line to the edge of each hip. You have now created an hourglass shape for the torso – the main part of the body.

From each hip, drop a further line into the spine to create a triangle. This marks the lower part of the torso.

IDEA

Imagine the shoulders as a coat hanger on which you are going to hang your favourite outfit.

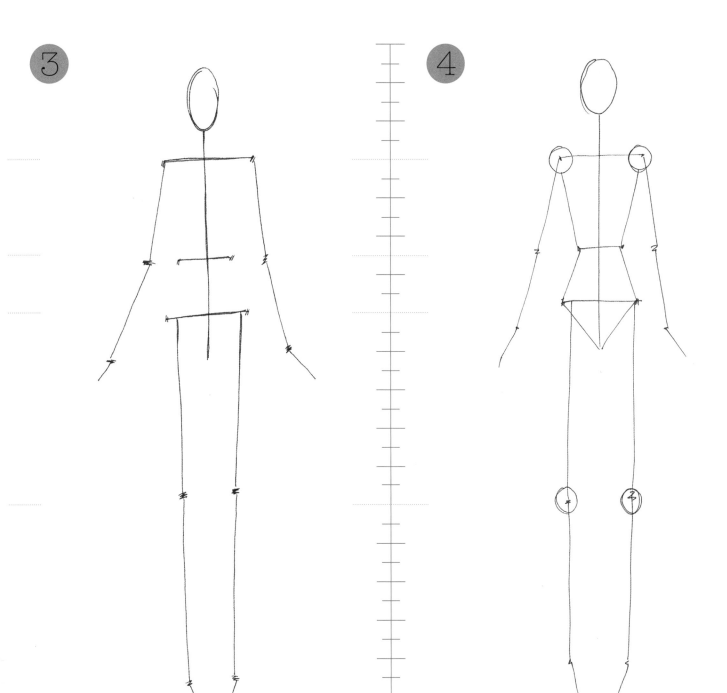

shoulders

waist

hips

knees

Thighs and calves

From the outside point of each hip, draw a smooth line to the outside of the kneecap. Then, from the lowest point of the torso drop a line to the inside of each kneecap. You have now drawn the thighs.

Draw a small circle to mark each ankle. Working from the outside of each knee to the outside of the ankle, create a shapely curve.

Create a similar curved line from the inside of each kneecap to each ankle. You have now drawn the lower legs.

IDEA

Drawing the calves takes practice. Be careful not to draw them wider than the thighs.

Neck and arms

From the head, drop down two lines to create the neck. Draw curved lines for the shoulders.

Add small circles at each elbow to show the joints. Now draw a line from the outside of each shoulder to the outside of each elbow joint. Draw a line from the inside of each shoulder to the inside of each elbow joint. You have drawn the upper arms.

To shape each forearm, draw a curved line from the outside of each elbow to each wrist point. To mirror this on the inside arm, draw a line from each inside elbow to each inside wrist.

IDEA

Look at your neck in the mirror to check out the shape of your shoulders. When you are drawing the forearms, look at your own forearms to see how they taper towards the wrists.

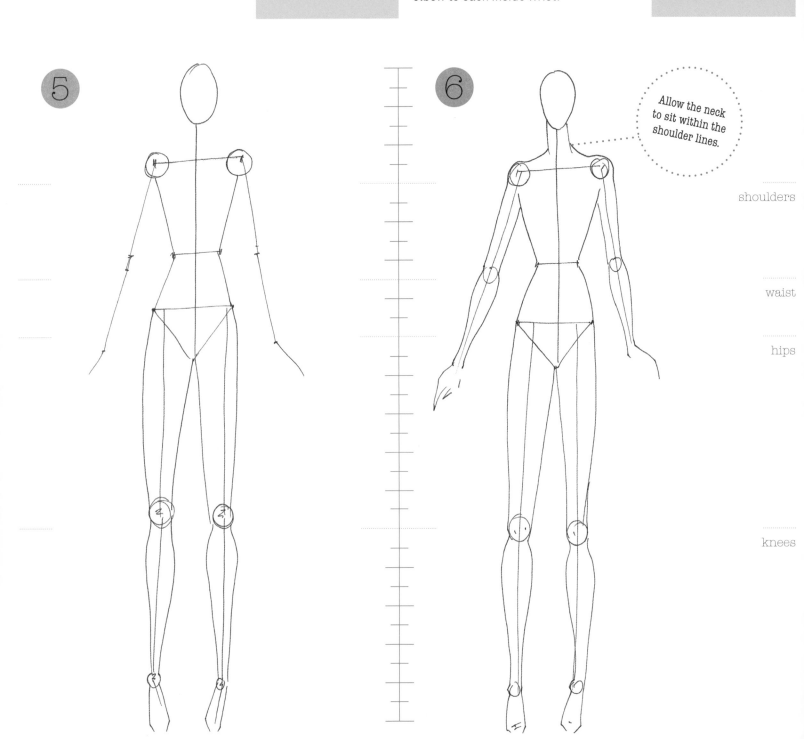

Allow the neck to sit within the shoulder lines.

shoulders

waist

hips

knees

Outline figure

At this point in the sequence you can remove the stick figure by tracing only the outline of your croquis.

Take a sheet of tracing paper or thin white paper, and place this over your step 6 drawing. Copy the outline.

IDEA

Remember that the best way to learn to draw a croquis is to practise drawing it again and again.

For speed, you could start designing clothes on a piece of paper placed over your croquis.

Creating definition

Now it's time to dress your croquis. The simplest garment is a swimsuit or leotard.

Think about how the fabric falls across the body by adding movement lines or stress lines, such as creases at the waist.

Marks at the joints give more definition. Add marks to highlight the knees, and two small marks for the collarbones just below the neck.

IDEA

Finish your croquis with simple facial features and add hair to suit your designs. Page 41 shows how to draw faces.

Not all fashion designers draw faces, so you can leave yours blank if you choose.

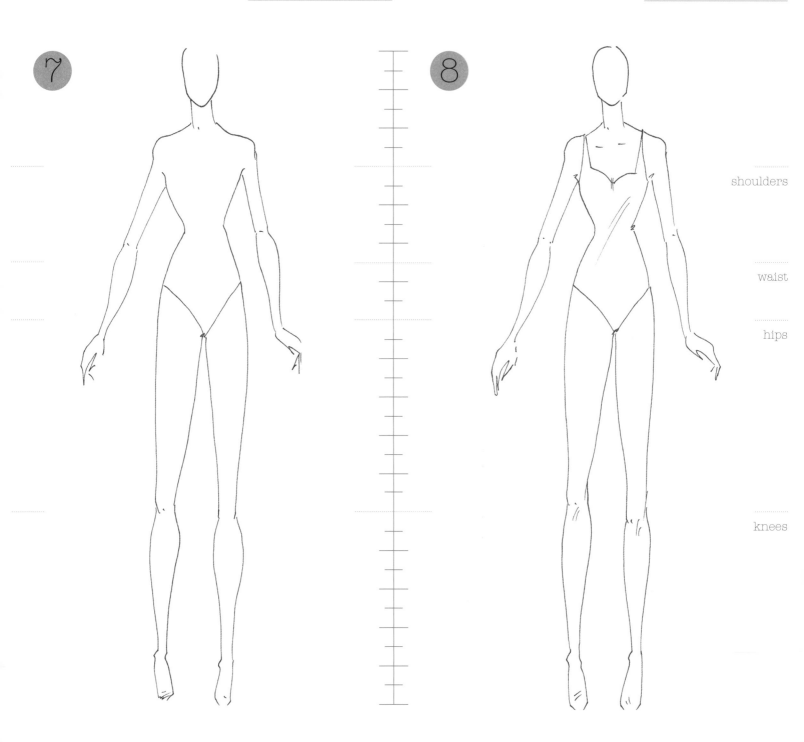

shoulders

waist

hips

knees

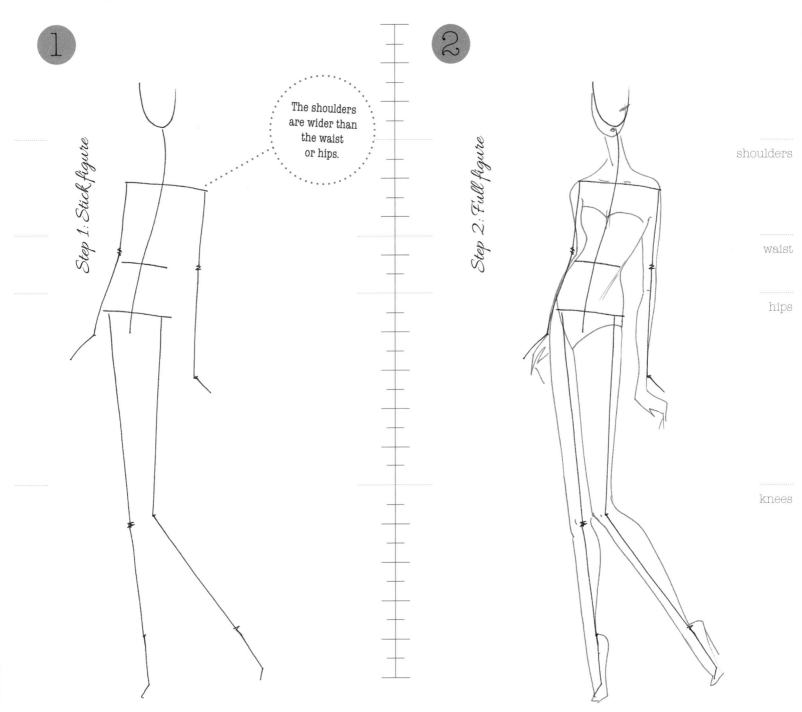

1

Step 1: Stick figure

The shoulders are wider than the waist or hips.

2

Step 2: Full figure

shoulders

waist

hips

knees

The stroll: step 1

When you have mastered the basic croquis, try out different poses to add variety to your designs.

For this pose, start with an oval head and a gently curving spine. Draw the shoulders, waist and hips at a slight angle. Drop a line for the left thigh. Mark the knee. Drop a line for the other thigh so that both knee joints almost touch. Continue both lines down to the ankles.

Draw the upper arms and forearms the same length, marking the elbows and wrists. Add hands and feet.

IDEA

Pay careful attention to proportions. Here, the spine should be at least three times as long as the head and each leg should measure at least five times the height of the head.

The stroll: step 2

Draw the torso with a line that starts at each shoulder and curves out around each hip. Draw a line in from each hip for the lower torso.

Draw the outside of both thighs. For the straight rear leg, continue this line to the foot. Draw a single line between the thighs. Working from the back of each knee to the ankle, create a shapely curve for the lower leg. Add a curve at each ankle point for the heel.

Drop two graceful lines on either side of the head for the neck and the top of each shoulder.

IDEA

Keep checking the proportions – for example, the calf should be narrower than the thigh. Remember that the outlines of the limbs should curve gently.

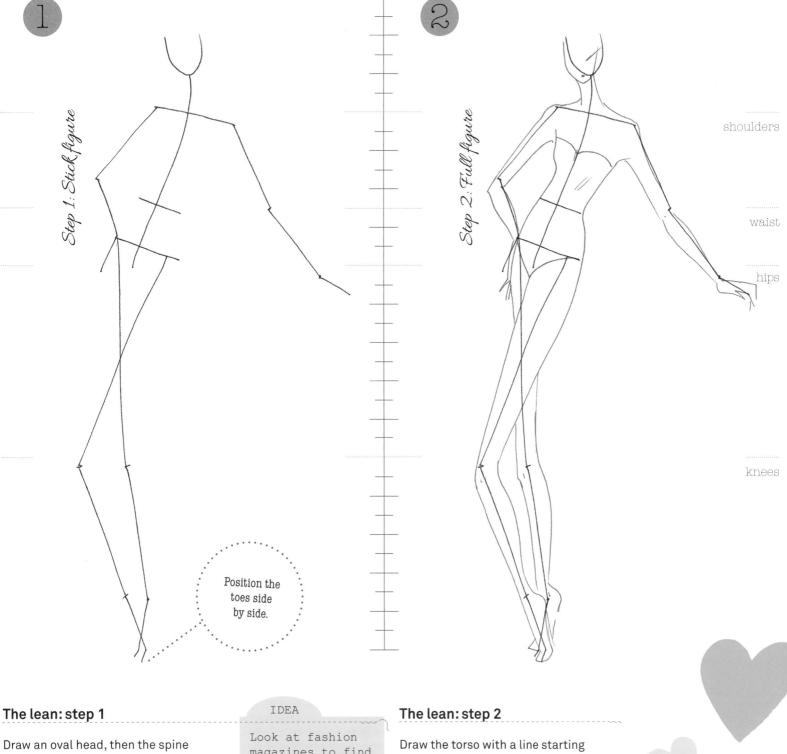

Step 1: Stick figure

Step 2: Full figure

Position the toes side by side.

shoulders

waist

hips

knees

The lean: step 1

Draw an oval head, then the spine with an exaggerated curve. Draw the shoulders, waist and hips at an angle across the spine.

Drop a line for the straight rear leg from the raised hip to the foot. Mark the knee and ankle. Drop a line for the bent leg from the lower hip to the knee, then continue to the ankle.

Draw the bent arm from the highest shoulder, then the outstretched arm. Mark the elbows and wrists.

IDEA

Look at fashion magazines to find models in poses you like. Trace the pose and draw lines for the spine, shoulder, waist and hips to help create a basic guide for your own fashion drawings.

The lean: step 2

Draw the torso with a line starting below each shoulder curving into the waist, then out around each hip. Draw a line in from each hip to create the lower torso.

Draw the silhouette, or shape, of the front leg first with curves for the thigh, calf and ankle. Fill in the leg behind.

Drop two graceful lines either side of the head for the neck and the top of each shoulder. Draw the silhouette of each arm.

Parts of the foot

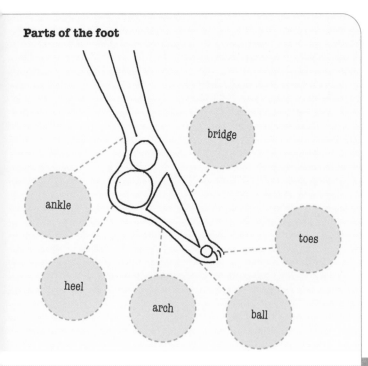

Remember that a foot measures the same length as the head. The ankle is a circle, the heel is a circle below and behind the ankle, the bridge is a triangle and the toes are an oval. The arch is the curved part of the sole. The ball is the widest part of the foot.

Two views of feet

For the forward-facing foot, draw a small circle for the ankle joint, then an oval for the foot. To draw a foot from the side, simplify the four key parts: ankle, heel, bridge and ball of the foot.

IDEA

When you start designing, it is easiest to position the figure and the feet facing forwards.

1

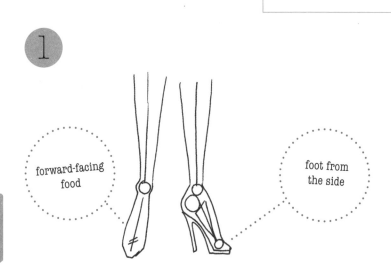

forward-facing food

foot from the side

Hand measurements

As with feet, you need to find a quick, simple solution to represent hands. Think about proportion. Outstretched hands are usually bigger than a person's face. The palm and the fingers measure approximately half a head each.

IDEA

Draw around your own hand in different positions. Include the wrist to see how much slimmer it is.

Hands in position

Keep your hands simple, leaving out details such as knuckles or fingernails. Consider the position too. A hand on a hip, in a pocket, or posed to one side can help to show your design off.

IDEA

Draw the hand holding an accessory such as a bag to add detail to your drawing.

2

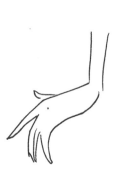

3

Facial features

Draw an oval for the head. Imagine a horizontal and vertical line crossing directly through the centre. Imagine another horizontal line dividing the lower face. Use these guidelines to help position the eyes, nose and lips.

The ideal face

Keep your faces simple so that you don't draw attention away from the clothes. Practise drawing eyes, eyebrows and lips – you could just hint at them with one or two lines, or even leave them out altogether.

Bobs and ponytails

For fashion drawing, you need to think of the hair as solid – imagine it as a plastic helmet on the head. Start with the outline shape and draw this around the head. The hairline usually begins a quarter-way down the head.

Waves and bunches

For curly hair, start with the outline. Then draw just a few wavy lines inside the outline to suggest curls. With more complicated styles, imagine them as simple shapes, then add a few lines to show the direction of the hair.

Where to start

Clothes can be grouped into a number of different categories, from dresses through to coats and accessories. The pages that follow show clothes designs organized into 12 different categories. To begin with, you may just want to copy them. But as you get more confident and develop your own style and ideas, you'll be able to come up with designs that are original to you – your own fashion collection.

1 dresses

2 skirts

3 shirts

4 knits

5 trousers

6 shorts

7 jackets

8 coats

9 party wear

10 necklines, pockets & cuffs

11 shoes & boots

12 bags & hats

Parts of a garment

It's useful to know the names for the different parts of a garment. You may already know some of them. In the two drawings below, you will see some familiar words and others that are perhaps new to you.

seam

collar

armhole

placket

cuff

waistband

neckline

lapel

bodice

dart

hem

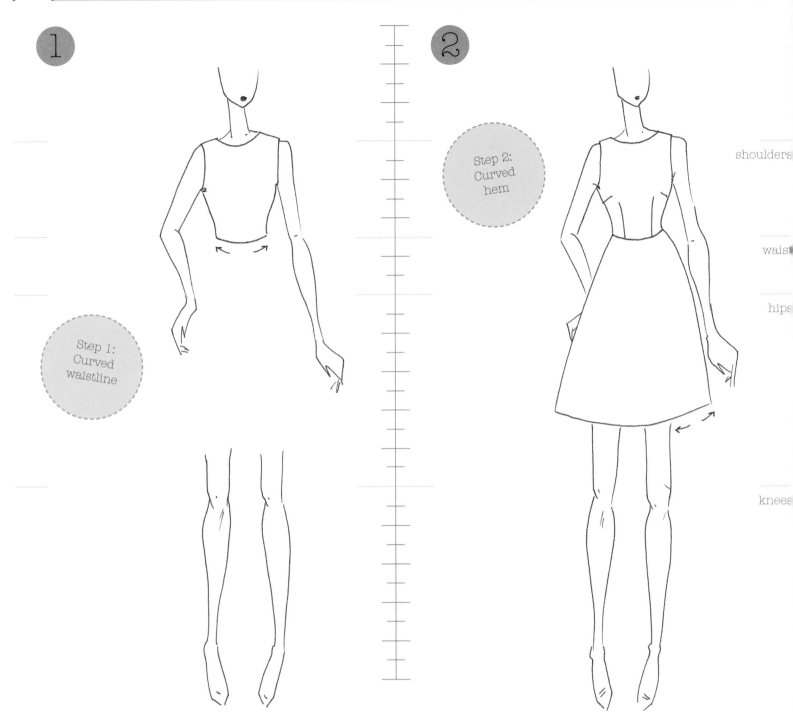

1

Step 1:
Curved
waistline

2

Step 2:
Curved
hem

shoulders

waist

hips

knees

Basic dress 1

Before you start designing, practise drawing this basic dress. It will give you an idea of what it is like to design around your croquis, or basic figure.

Start with a simple round neck. Follow the shape of the shoulders to create the shoulder seams. Draw a gentle curve for the waistband. Draw lines from the waistband up to the armpits for the sides of the dress.

For each armhole, draw a line from beneath the armpit to the shoulder.

IDEA

Always start from your basic croquis. You can draw a new croquis each time or trace over an earlier one. If you are tracing, don't draw over the parts of the body that are covered by fabric.

Basic dress 2

Now add four darts to shape the bodice.

Add the skirt, starting from the waistband. Dresses do not always need to be fitted but, when you're learning to draw, it helps to see where the waist sits. In this dress, the skirt has a simple flared shape. This is called an A-line.

Give the hem a gentle curve.

IDEA

Experiment with different shapes of skirt on your dress. You can make them very full or closely fitting the body.

Darts help to shape this dress below the bust.

A-line dress

This is a version of the basic dress but it has a flared shape.

First draw the neck and then the armholes.

Start from under one arm and draw a line that flares out to the hem. Do the same on the other side.

Draw darts for the bust under the arms. Draw two darts near the waist.

Draw a gentle curve for the hem.

IDEA

It's good to show details of how a garment has been put together so that it fits different parts of the body. Darts are one way of shaping a garment.

Dropped waist dress

This is another version of the basic dress but it has a dropped waist.

Start with a V-shaped neckline. Draw the dropped waistline as a gentle curve that runs from the top of one hip to the top of the other.

Follow the shape of the waist closely to give a nipped-in look to the sides of the dress.

Add two darts to shape the waist. Finish with a simple flared skirt.

IDEA

Experiment with the length of the bodice and change the silhouette, or outline shape. Make the skirt straight or fuller, and decide where to attach this to the bodice.

Use scribbly lines for the gathers in the sleeves

shoulders

waist

hips

knees

Waisted dress

Start with a scooped neckline and add a frill below it.

Draw in the bodice, then add the waistband.

Create a nice full skirt to finish just above the knee. Add a curved hem with a frill below.

IDEA

Frills are a useful detail for highlighting necklines and hemlines. Make sure the frills stick out at the shoulders and at the sides of the hem to make them look three-dimensional.

Empire-line dress

Draw a scooped neckline and add puffed sleeves that rise slightly above the shoulder joints.

Draw the edges of the bodice to meet a seam just below the bust.

Hang the A-line skirt from this seam. To make the skirt look full, draw lines in it to suggest folds in the fabric and use a wavy line for the hem.

IDEA

This style is called 'empire' after the French Empress Joséphine, who first made it popular. To learn more about this type of design, look back at fashions of the late 18th and early 19th centuries.

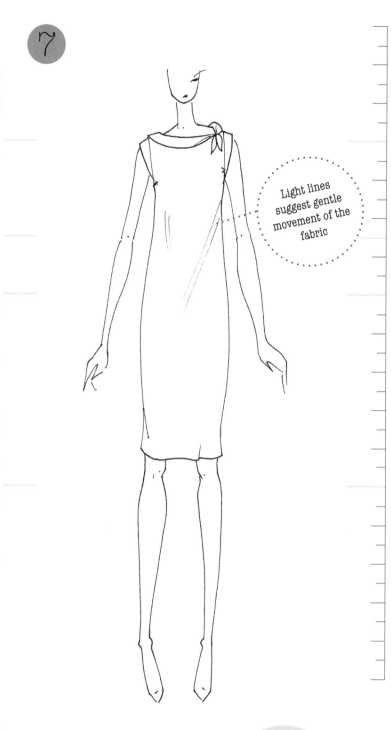

7

Light lines suggest gentle movement of the fabric

No-waist dress

Draw two gently curved lines across the collarbone to create a shallow neckline. Add a bow to one side for the fastening.

Hang the dress from the collar by drawing a line from the edge of each shoulder running straight down to just above the knee.

Give the hemline a very shallow curve.

Add a flare at each shoulder to create the capped sleeves.

IDEA

This simple silhouette, or shape, is also known as a sheath or sack dress. It became popular in the 1950s. To see more sheath dresses, look especially at the work of Cristobal Balenciaga.

Try this: drawing hems

Your designs will look more real if you show how the fabric in the skirt gathers and folds.

1 Draw lines down from the waistband to show where the gathers or pleats fall.

2 Join the fabric at the hem. Use a shallow curve between each pleat, curving inwards then outwards.

3 To create a ruffled hem, add a frill to the bottom of the skirt. The frill should stick out at the sides. Use gather lines to show how the fabric folds where the frill joins the skirt. Draw folds at the hem too.

4 With a skirt cut on the bias, or diagonal, the fullness of the fabric falls at the bottom not the top. Start the gather lines close to the bottom of the skirt. Join these at the hem with curves that go in and out. Dress 8 on page 48 tells you more about the bias cut.

8

The seam shows where the fabric is cut on the diagonal.

9

A bow on one side draws attention to the neckline.

shoulders

waist

hips

knees

Bias-cut dress

Draw two straps from the inside of each shoulder to just above the bust.

Draw a curved line between the straps for the neckline and continue the line under the arms.

Draw in the silhouette of the dress to follow the shape of the body but let it flare out at the hem.

IDEA

Bias-cut dresses use fabric that is cut on a diagonal, which gives the fabric greater stretch. To create a dress that closely follows the shape of the body yet still allows for movement, go for a bias-cut design.

Tunic dress

For the neckline, draw a line across from one shoulder to the other.

For the armholes, draw a line straight down from each edge of the neckline.

Now draw the sides of the dress. Add sleeves that follow the arms on your basic figure.

IDEA

Top-stitching is a decorative line of stitches on the outside of a garment. It's a great way to draw attention to parts of a design, for example, the neckline, cuffs and hem.

10

Rolled-up sleeves emphasize the casual style of this dress.

11

shoulders

waist

hips

Wavy folds at the hemline suggest the fullness of the skirt.

knees

Shirt dress

For the neckline, draw a small, tight V-shape, ending just below the base of the neck. Draw the collar around it.

Draw the outline of the bodice – the top of the dress – and the skirt, loosely following the outline of the body.

From the base of the V draw a line straight to the hem. Add buttons alongside this line, from just below the collar to halfway down the skirt.

Add a tie-belt and draw the sleeves.

IDEA

Think how you can change the look of this basic shirt dress by varying the detailing, such as the belt and buttons. How would it look with a fuller skirt?

Wrap dress

Start with the collar on the left. Draw the outside edge first, then the inner edge. Take this inner line diagonally down to the right side of the waistline, to create the wrap.

Draw the other side of the collar in the same way, to form a V-shape.

Draw the shoulders, then add the armholes, continuing these lines down to meet the waist.

Add the sash, and finish with a full skirt and neat sleeves.

IDEA

For more inspiration on wrap dresses, look at the work of American designer Diane von Furstenberg. This relaxed, easy-fitting style is closely associated with her work.

Wrap skirt

Draw a narrow waistband across the top of the skirt. Continue it diagonally across and add a string tie. Now draw both sides of the skirt. Drop a gently angled line from the string tie down to the hem. Draw in the hem.

IDEA

To show that there are two layers of fabric, give your skirt a split hemline, with a longer front flap.

Tulip skirt

Start with a wide waistband. Draw a diagonal line from the right side of the waist down to the opposite corner of the skirt. Following the curves of the body, draw in the sides, then join them up with a diagonal line at the hem.

IDEA

Shade the small section inside the bottom of the skirt to show that this is the inside of the fabric.

waist

hips

Top-stitching along the edges emphasizes the wrap.

knees

Small, neat buttons draw attention to the waist.

waist

hips

knees

Pleated skirt

Draw the waistband. Then bring your pleat lines straight down from it at regular intervals, angling them slightly. Finish the pleats with a zigzag edge at the hem to indicate the folds in the fabric.

IDEA

Try varying the width of your pleats according to the fabric – the thicker the fabric, the bigger the pleats.

Bell skirt

Draw a simple, curved waistband. Then add the sides of the skirt, giving the skirt a bell shape. Draw a loose, wavy hemline to show that there is movement in the fabric.

IDEA

For a different style of bell skirt, try giving your design a narrower hem.

waist

hips

knees

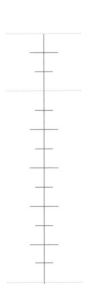

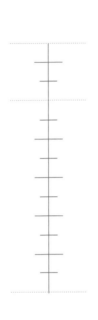

waist

hips

knees

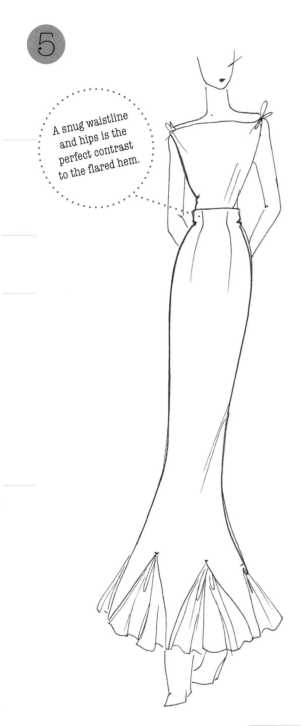

5

A snug waistline and hips is the perfect contrast to the flared hem.

Try this: different lengths

Just altering the length turns a mini-skirt into the pencil skirt on the right.

Godet skirt

Starting from a high waist, draw the outline of a long skirt. Let the outline follow the shape of the hips until just below the knee, where it should flare out. Add triangles of gathered fabric at the bottom of the skirt. Make the hemline uneven to show the fullness of the fabric.

IDEA

This skirt gets its name from 'godet' (pronouned *go-day*), which is a triangular piece of fabric. Adding godets – especially to dresses, shirts and gloves – is one way to add a flare to a fitted garment.

There are a number of classic skirt shapes such as the circle, A-line, pencil and kilt. You can create different skirt designs just by varying these shapes or combining different features.

The tulip shape of skirt 2 on page 50 combines a slim, pencil skirt with a wrapover. Try making it fuller by giving it more of a bell shape, like skirt 4. To create a kilt, use the basic shape of skirt 3 but give it a flat wrapover panel at the front.

You can also alter the character of a skirt by varying the length and style of the waistband.

Try varying the skirts you add to your dresses, too, to see how many different looks you can achieve.

1

The sleeves have overlapping caps.

2

A little tuck shows where the neck opening ends.

shoulders

waist

hips

knees

Cap-sleeve T-shirt

Draw a short straight line across the base of the neck. Then draw the top of the T-shirt, taking the lines out just beyond the edge of the shoulders.

Add the armholes so that they drop down wide of the shoulders. Add two little triangles for the cap sleeves.

Now draw two vertical lines down from the armholes for the sides of the T-shirt. Join with a gently wavy line across the bottom, to give a boxy shape.

IDEA

Think about what to pair this T-shirt with. The straight skirt here has a similar boxy shape. How would it look paired with very different shapes – say, a bell skirt or full trousers?

Collarless shirt

Draw a narrow, upright collar. For the front opening, draw a narrow slit down from the centre of the collar to just above the bust.

Draw in the armholes and continue these lines down for the sides of the shirt, gently following the shape of the body underneath. Fill in the hem.

Add loose sleeves with cuffs. Add a collar button and buttonhole. Finish with top-stitching at the neckline and hem.

IDEA

When designing your shirt, think about where it will be worn. Should it be loose for informal occasions and hot weather – like the shirt here – or fitted and more formal?

③

This placket, or opening, is bound with a strip of fabric.

④

shoulders

waist

hips

knees

Basic button-down shirt

Draw the collar so it curves around the neck, but leave a little gap to show that it is not fitted.

Draw the opening in the shirt, which is known as the placket, from the left collar down to the waist. Draw the other side of the placket to create a V-shaped neck opening.

Add gently curved armholes and long, loose sleeves with cuffs. Finish by drawing in the sides of the shirt. Don't forget to suggest the gathers in the fabric.

IDEA

Try adding top-stitching to highlight the shoulder and armhole seams. Add buttons to the placket or leave them hidden behind it. Remember that even practical details can be decorative features too.

Wrap shirt

Draw the left side of the collar and drop a line down diagonally from it to the waist. Complete the other side of the neckline to create a V-shape.

Draw the left side of the shirt, then the right. Add a gathered waistband, with a big bow on one hip. Add lines to show how the shirt pulls in at the waist.

Add the sleeves – loose ones will go best with this style of shirt.

IDEA

The big bow at the waist is a strong feature of this design. To keep the focus on the bow, it's best to pair the shirt with a simple skirt.

Round-neck jumper

Draw a gentle curve for the neckline. Add the shoulders and armholes. Continue the line of each armhole down to the hips, following the outline of the body. Add short sleeves and detailing at the hem.

shoulders

waist

hips

Twin set

Add a cardigan to round-neck jumper 1. Both necklines need to match. Finish the necklines, cuffs and hems with bands of rib stitch. Ribbing will make these edges more stretchy and will help them to hold their shape.

shoulders

waist

hips

V-neck jumper

This classic style of jumper is characterized by its V-neck. Draw it like round-neck jumper 1, but give it a V-shaped neckline. Add ribbing at the neck, cuffs and hem to highlight them.

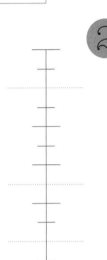

shoulders

waist

hips

Polo-neck jumper

Knits like this, with a high, upright neck, are also known as turtlenecks. Mock turtlenecks are a softer, less upright version. Draw this polo neck like V-neck jumper 3, but make the shape softer and less fitting.

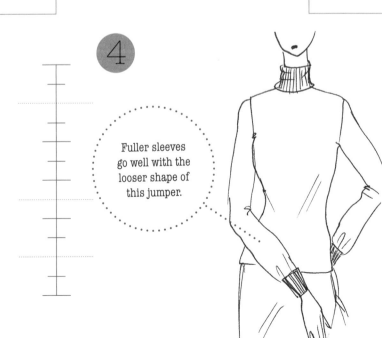

Fuller sleeves go well with the looser shape of this jumper.

shoulders

waist

hips

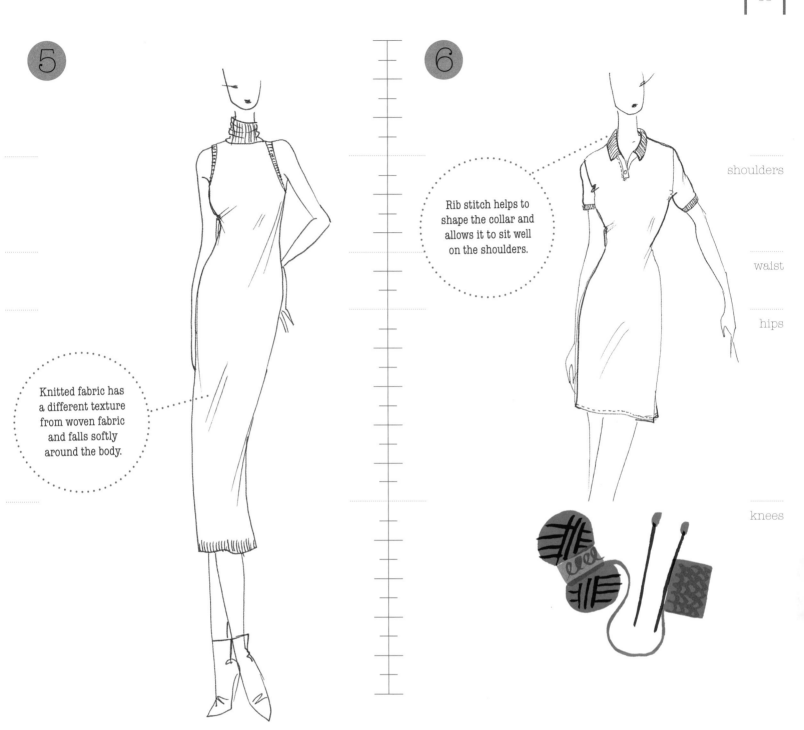

5

Knitted fabric has a different texture from woven fabric and falls softly around the body.

6

Rib stitch helps to shape the collar and allows it to sit well on the shoulders.

shoulders

waist

hips

knees

Sleeveless sweater dress

Sweater dresses are usually associated with colder weather and fairly thick yarn, so this sleeveless dress is a bit of a surprise.

Start with a polo neck, then draw armholes angled diagonally outwards into the armpits to show off the shoulders.

Complete the outline of the dress so that it gently follows the shape of the body without being too clingy. Finish with the ribbing at the neck, armholes and hem to show that this is a knit.

IDEA

How else could you vary this simple design? A chunky belt around the waist could look good, or perhaps you could play with different styles of sleeve.

Polo dress

This is a variation on the V-neck, with a roll collar and a soft placket, or opening. Starting with the collar, draw in a short placket with a small V. Draw in the shoulder lines, the armholes and the outline of the dress, letting it gently follow the shape of the body.

Add short sleeves to finish halfway above the elbows. Complete the detailing at collar and cuffs, placket and hem.

IDEA

Don't make your drawings too complicated but do make sure they contain the essential features of your design. Here, the ribbed collar and cuffs are important because they help to define the style.

shoulders

waist

hips

knees

A loosely buckled belt pulls in the baggy waistline.

Skinny jeans

Draw the waistband, curving the double line to show that the band fits tightly around the body. Draw the outline of the left leg: add the outer side first, then fill in the inside leg, following the body shape closely. Repeat for the right leg.

Draw the pockets. Add the seams – from the centre of the waist, along the outside of one leg, and along the inside of the other leg. Finish with top-stitching detail.

IDEA

Rivets and top-stitching are typical of denim garments. They help to hold this hard-wearing fabric together, but they can also be a decorative detail – so have fun with them.

Boyfriend jeans

This is a similar trouser shape to the skinny jeans but with a much looser fit. Draw a slightly wavy line for the waistband, just below the waist, to show that it sits loosely on the hips. Add two diagonal lines for the pockets, starting at the waistband.

Draw the legs, adding the outside lines first. Add cuffs at the hem, and finish with some top-stitching along the pocket slits and the placket.

IDEA

Make sure the legs of these jeans are straight and loose – boyfriend jeans are meant to look as if they were designed for a man.

3

Darts are essential for a smooth waistline.

Cropped pants

Start with a high waistline and continue it down into the trouser outline, following the basic figure shape. Decide how much of the trouser you want to crop. Add a little slit in each hem to allow for extra movement.

This type of trouser is rarely made out of denim, which needs strong stitching, so the top-stitching here is just a decorative feature. Add detailing for buttons at the hem depending on how fitted the legs are.

IDEA

Think of a special name for your cropped pants that goes with the theme of your collection. For a contrast in shape, pair them with a wide, cropped sweater.

Try this: different trouser shapes

Made fashionable by film stars from the 1930s onwards, there are now a huge variety of trouser designs including: slim-leg, cropped-leg, peg, pleated, palazzo, jodhpurs, bloomers, bootcut, button-ankle, bellbottoms, kick-flare, Oxford bags, churidar, leggings, ski and jogging pants. Research these different shapes to see which you like.

Before you start to draw, think about the silhouette, or shape, of your trousers and what they are designed for. Look at the first design above. These jodhpurs are designed for horseriding, so they are wide on the hips and narrow on the legs. The baggy trousers next to them are really comfortable and great for everyday wear.

⑤

⑥

A full-sleeved, frilly blouse contrasts nicely with the smooth shape of the trousers.

A neat fitted jacket emphasizes the fuller, wider shape of the trousers.

shoulders

waist

hips

knees

High-waisted trousers

Draw a line above the waist, just below the bust. Add darts to show the trousers are fitted at the waistline and hips.

Follow the edge of your basic figure around the outside of the hips. Continue the lines from here straight down to create the wide legs. Draw the inner line between the two legs. Curve the hem slightly.

Add buttons down the middle of the waistband to highlight this part of the design.

IDEA

Remember that the fuller the trouser leg is, the more curved the hemline should be – avoid straight hemlines on trousers!

Wide-legged trousers

Draw the waistband and hang the outer lines of the trousers straight down from the waist. Imagine the fabric falling away from the body to create a wider silhouette. The hems should be widely curved.

Add slanting pockets, with stitching detail for emphasis.

IDEA

For inspiration, look at pictures of the actress Katherine Hepburn and the designs of Coco Chanel. Both helped to make trousers popular as a fashion item for women.

7

8

Cuffed hems are an interesting detail.

Classic trousers

This classic trouser shape has a fitted waistband and belt loops. Start from the waistband as usual. Don't forget the cutaway pockets as you draw down the outline of each leg.

Add the placket opening at the top of the trousers, and draw in front pleats to give each leg more shape. Complete the drawing with cuffs at the hem.

A belt, slotted through loops around the waistband, is a nice finishing touch.

IDEA

When drawing a cuffed hem, make sure that you make it slightly wider than the trouser leg to show how the fabric is folded back on itself.

Low-waisted trousers

The low-slung waistline and gathered-in ankles are what define this design.

Draw the top of the trousers just below the waist. Draw both legs, gathering them in at the ankles.

Add crease lines at each ankle to indicate where the fabric gathers.

IDEA

A pose like this is good for showing off trousers. The bent knee and three-quarter view of the right leg allow you to see the shape of the trouser leg more clearly. You can also see the way the fabric folds at the knee.

Sports shorts

Playing sports is easy in these loose-fitting shorts. Draw the waistband at a slight angle, just below the waist, then complete the outline. Don't forget the V-shaped notch at the bottom of the side seam, to give even more movement.

IDEA

Imagine these shorts without the practical drawstring – and you'll see how practical details can also be decorative.

Cut-off denim shorts

These shorts are made by cutting the legs off a pair of jeans. Give them a similar outline to the sports shorts on the left, but make the legs straighter. Add curved pockets, a placket and a button fastening.

IDEA

The legs of cut-off denim shorts can be any length. Try the same design with legs that stop just above the knee.

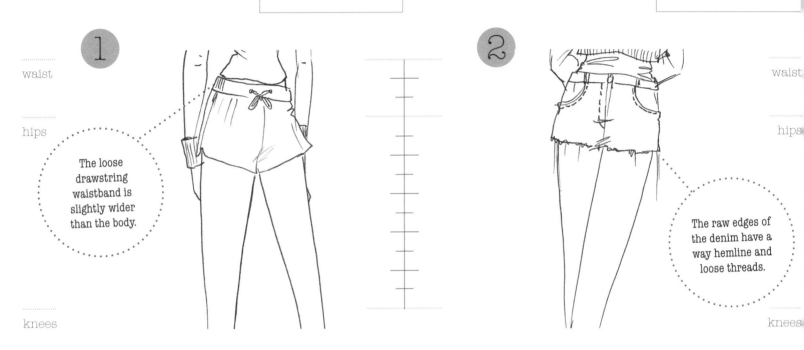

waist

hips

The loose drawstring waistband is slightly wider than the body.

knees

waist

hips

The raw edges of the denim have a way hemline and loose threads.

knees

Bermuda shorts

This style was first worn by the British Army in hot climates and became especially popular in Bermuda, which is how the shorts got their name. This design follows the classic trouser shape, with creases down the front.

IDEA

How could you add interest to this very simple shape? Perhaps the shorts could be made up in a brightly patterned fabric.

Cargo shorts

With fashion garments, details are more often used for decoration rather than for practical reasons. This example features two styles of pocket. It has drawstrings at the hem and the waist as a design feature.

IDEA

The practical 'cargo' pockets that give these shorts their name are also a key design feature of the style.

waist

hips

knees

waist

hips

Cargo pockets can be placed almost anywhere on the legs.

knees

Culottes

Think of culottes as a skirt that has been split in two. Draw the waistband, side pockets and A-line shape. Then draw the inner leg line, and give each leg a curved hem to show how the culottes are made up.

Look back at the skirt of the basic dress on page 44 to help you draw the A-line outline of these culottes.

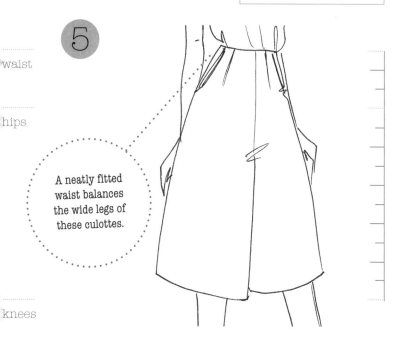

⑤

waist

hips

A neatly fitted waist balances the wide legs of these culottes.

knees

Pedal pushers

IDEA

Start with a high waistband and draw a smooth outline, following the shape of the body. Add the central seam and waistline darts for a neat fit. Notice the little slit seam at the hem – this allows for greater movement

Be inventive when naming your designs. These 'pedal pushers' got their name because they were worn by the first women cyclists.

⑥

waist

hips

Buttons at the waist and hem add interest to this simple design.

knees

Try this: varying the detail

These hot pants have a sporty, boyish feel.

These high-waisted shorts look more feminine than the hot pants.

The shorts on these two pages look different from each other because of their length, style of waist and details. Think how you could alter the same basic silhouette by varying these features. Think, too, about whether you want your shorts to be casual, sporty or dressy.

The two designs above have similar shapes but the length and detailing give each one a different 'feel'.

These simple hot pants, with their very short legs and cuffs, are meant for casual wear. By making the legs longer and adding a high waist, buttons, top-stitching and a ribbon belt, these high-waisted shorts are a more complicated design and look more dressy.

Fish-eye darts pull the fabric in at the waist.

shoulders

waist

hips

knees

Double-breasted jacket

Start with the collar which has a notched lapel. Draw the top part, followed by the second part.

Now draw a line down from the left lapel and continue it down to become the jacket opening.

Draw the shoulders and the armholes, then the body of the jacket. Add the sleeves, a double line for the binding on each pocket, and buttons.

IDEA

For a really fitted shape, use fish-eye darts. To make a fish-eye dart, you cut out a diamond shape from the fabric. This will leave a diamond-shaped hole. You then sew the edges of the hole together, to pull the fabric in tight.

Shawl-collar jacket

This style of jacket suits more formal dressing. Draw the left side of the collar so that the inner line comes down to form the front opening. Add the other side of the collar. This is a smooth collar so keep the line even – there are no notches in the lapel.

Draw in the shoulders so that they drop slightly out beyond the body. Add the armholes and continue these lines down the side of the jacket to create a loose shape.

To finish, add the sleeves and the buttons.

IDEA

Shawl-collar lapels are usually in a different fabric from the rest of the jacket. Use shading to show this.

Hacking jackets often have a two-part collar, made of velvet and tweed.

Hacking jacket

This style of jacket is often associated with sports such as riding.

Start with the two parts of the collar. Continue the inner line of the left-hand collar down to form the front opening. Add the shoulders and the body, including bust darts and fish-eye darts at the waist to show the close fit.

Draw in closely fitting sleeves. Highlight the front fastening with a single set of buttons. The different pockets are key design features – show them with pocket flaps and double lines.

IDEA

Use shading for the velvet part of the collar to show that it is different from the tweed part.

Try this: single-breasted or double-breasted?

This single-breasted jacket is pulled in at the waist for a curvy shape.

This double-breasted jacket is more boxy in shape.

Here are two suggestions for how your jacket will fasten: a two-button single-breasted jacket and a six-button double-breasted one. Play around to see how many buttons will suit your design.

Think about the hem of the jacket too. The first illustration shows a cutaway hem and the double-breasted jacket has a square hem. But you could also consider a round regular hem too.

Don't forget that women's and men's clothes fasten on opposite sides. Women's traditionally fasten right over left, and men's clothes left over right – but no one can remember why!

4

5

A button flap at the cuff adds extra detail.

Pea coat

Pea coats were originally worn by sailors and fishermen. They are usually double-breasted and boxy in shape. The wide collar is practical too – it can be pulled up to ward off harsh weather.

Start with the collar, drawing it as wide as possible. Draw the jacket to fall well outside the body shape.

Add sleeves that widen nearer the cuff. Include details such as pocket stitching and big buttons.

> **IDEA**
>
> For a classic touch, choose buttons with an anchor motif or some other nautical design.

Boyfriend jacket

This style of jacket is usually worn open, for a cool, casual look.

Start with a notched collar with open lapels. Continue the line of each lapel down the front of the body to the hips.

Draw the armholes, the sides of the jacket and the sleeves. Add pockets and two small buttons and buttonholes at the waistline.

Short darts at the bust and the waist mould the jacket slightly to the body.

> **IDEA**
>
> This jacket is strictly informal – so roll up the sleeves for a really relaxed look. Team it with a short skirt or jeans.

Bolero

Draw in a small, tight, upright collar that drops straight down into the front opening. Add the shoulders, then the armholes, continuing the lines down to form the sides of the jacket. Add fitted sleeves.

IDEA

Boleros are often worn with evening wear. For a bit of evening glamour, add some beading and embroidery.

Dolman-sleeve jacket

The sleeves and body of this jacket are cut from one piece of fabric. Follow the outer line of the shoulders and arms to create the outline, then complete the inner arms. Gather the fabric in to a wide waistband.

IDEA

For a really flattering shape, go for dolman sleeves – they make the waist look much narrower than the shoulders.

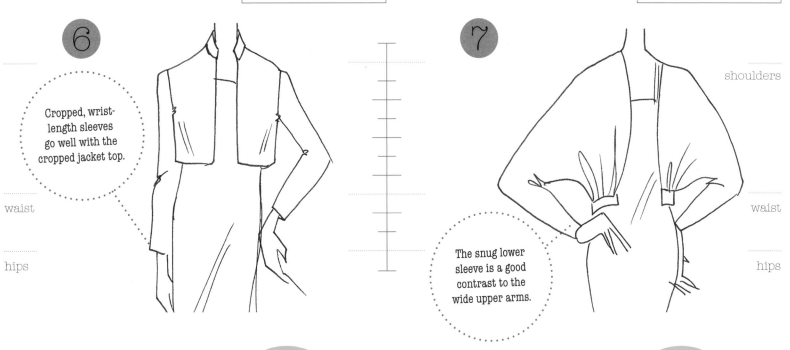

6

Cropped, wrist-length sleeves go well with the cropped jacket top.

waist

hips

7

shoulders

waist

hips

The snug lower sleeve is a good contrast to the wide upper arms.

Swing coat

Draw the collar. Add the shoulders and armholes with a tiny notch to show how the fabric pulls under the arm. Draw the sides flaring out to the hips. Add the front opening and a wavy hemline. Add the arms, pockets and buttons.

IDEA

It doesn't matter how wide you draw the flare of the coat – it's the number of folds at the hem that shows how full the fabric is.

Biker jacket

This style of jacket is typically made from leather, with lots of detailing. Draw the collar first, then the arms and the body. Add other details to complete the look – a diagonal zip at the neck, zips on the cuffs and a belted waistband.

IDEA

Leather comes only in small pieces so leather clothes usually have more seams – make the most of this in your design.

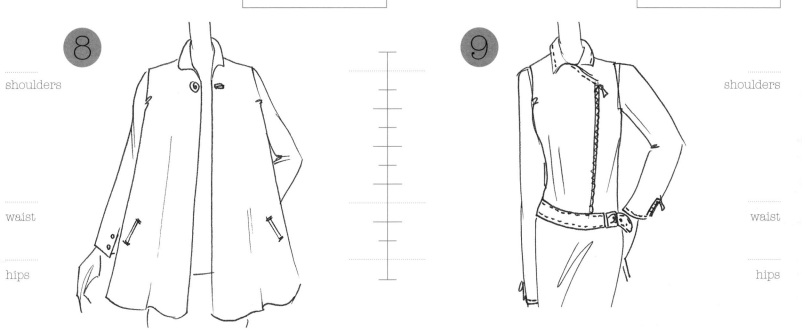

8

shoulders

waist

hips

9

shoulders

waist

hips

1

Shading shows the parts that are made of velvet.

2

This collar is called a funnel-neck because it is shaped like a funnel.

shoulders

waist

hips

knees

Chesterfield coat

Draw the two-part collar – start with a long V-shaped neckline and then add the lapels or revers. Add the shoulders.

Now draw the outline of the coat. Follow the basic figure closely at the waist and hips for a fitted shape, but let the skirt flare out at the knees. You can make the skirt longer if you like.

Draw the sleeves, then add buttons and low pockets that sit on the hips.

> **IDEA**
>
> A Chesterfield coat usually has a velvet collar, but it can be single- or double-breasted. Page 63 tells you more about this.

Funnel-neck coat

Draw a stand-up collar with a tight curved line around the neck. Add a dart on either side to create the funnel shape.

Draw a line straight down the centre of your basic figure to the hips, for the front opening. Add the left shoulder and a low armhole. Complete the outline of the jacket to meet the centre fastening.

Do the same for the right side of the coat. Add the sleeves, plus details for the pockets and fastening.

> **IDEA**
>
> This coat has a hidden placket with the seam and zip pull showing. Try other types of fastening, such as buttons or poppers.

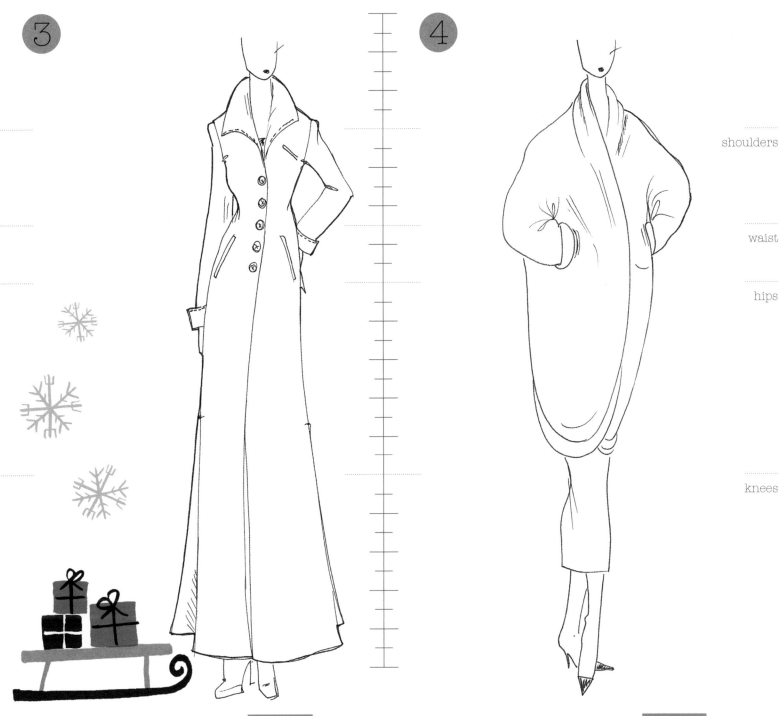

shoulders

waist

hips

knees

Greatcoat

Starting just below the point where the neck joins the head, draw the curved outside edge of one side of the collar.

Now draw the curved bottom edge, then draw the inside of the collar. Continue this line all the way down the centre of the coat to the ankles.

Draw the other side of the collar in the same way. Create the body of the coat – make it fitted at the waist but let the skirt flare out. Add sleeves and the other details.

IDEA

Have fun with the typical features of the greatcoat – deep pockets, big, warm collars and cuffs, and epaulettes, or shoulder straps.

Cocoon coat

This coat has no fastening. Start with the neckline, draw a long S-shape down the centre of the basic figure. It should be narrow at the neck and wide at the hem.

Add a soft collar with lines curving out from behind the neck, then following the neckline. Draw the shoulders and arms. Add a curved hem on both sides.

Finish with some lines to show the movement of the fabric as it is pulled in to create the cocoon shape.

IDEA

Team your cosy, round cocoon coat with a pencil-line skirt or narrow trousers, for a contrast in shape.

①

Scribbly lines are a good way to suggest lace.

②

A sweetheart neckline is shaped like the top of a heart.

shoulders

waist

hips

knees

Lace dress

Draw the bodice first, starting with the straps. Draw a heart-shaped neckline. Add the edges of the bodice and a seam below the bustline.

Hang the gathered skirt from the seam. Draw lines to suggest the fabric folds.

Draw the higher hemline using uneven curves between the fabric folds. Draw another hemline below this to show the two layers of fabric.

IDEA

This pretty frock is ideal for a teenage party. How would the mood alter if you gave it a longer bodice and skirt? Would it suit a different age group - or a different event?

Flapper dress

Draw two straps from the inside of each shoulder to just above the bust. Add a scooped neckline between the straps, taking this line under each arm. Draw a sweetheart neckline above this to show the slip underneath the dress.

Complete the outline of the dress, giving it a wavy 'handkerchief' hemline.

Use fine, scribbly lines to create an embroidered pattern at the neckline, hips and hem.

IDEA

In the 1920s, fashion changed dramatically - hemlines rose, waists dropped and 'boyish' figures became fashionable. Girls who wore the daring new styles were known as 'flappers'. Look at 1920s fashion for more inspiration.

③

④

A strapless dress needs to be held in place with boning or elastic.

Cocktail dress

Draw a long V from the centre of each shoulder to just above the waist. Add lines for the shoulders, taking them out beyond the body. Then draw the armholes, continuing the lines to just above the waist.

Add a wide, tight waistband. Draw the skirt shape so that it flares out at the hips and then drops down to just above the knees.

Use thin, shaded ovals to show how the fabric gathers between the waist and hips.

IDEA

Think about how the different parts of a dress or an outfit work together. Here, the width of the skirt at the hips balances the wide shoulder pads – and both make the waistline look really tiny.

Strapless dress

Draw the lower neckline with two lines that meet in the middle of the bust area. Draw two pleats above this for the inner bodice.

Add the sides of the bodice and a wide waistband, with a bow for detail.

Draw a full shape for the skirt, making it stand away from the sides of the body. Don't forget the lines in the bodice and the skirt that show how the fabric gathers into the waistband.

IDEA

For formal evening wear, think about the length of the skirt. Evening dresses or ball gowns are usually full-length, ballerina-length, which stops above the ankle, or tea-length, which stops at mid-calf.

Boat neck

The French designer Coco Chanel made the boat neck popular in women's fashion. She took the idea from the wide necks that French sailors wore. Draw a shallow curve from one shoulder to the other, just above the collarbone.

IDEA

The traditional boat-neck tops that French sailors wore had horizontal stripes. Try adding these to your design.

Sweetheart neck

Draw a curved line from the middle of each shoulder down to just above the bust. Join with a heart-shaped neckline, centred above the bust. Add the outside edges of the straps, plus a line to indicate the cleavage.

IDEA

Experiment with different shoulder straps, such as halter-neck or very thin 'spaghetti' straps.

1

waist

2

This low-cut shape works well on a fitted bodice.

shoulders

waist

Off-the-shoulder collar

Draw a shallow curve, starting just below one shoulder to a point below the other shoulder. Add another curve between the neckline and bustline to create the the off-the-shoulder collar.

IDEA

Think about adding details such as a frill or bow to the neckline, particularly if this is part of a dress design.

Cowl neck

Starting on one side of the neck, draw a long curve that runs below the bust line and back up to the middle of the other shoulder. Create the inner cowl shape in the same way. Add a straight line above the bust.

IDEA

Make sure you add plenty of folds in your design – a cowl neck is very full.

3

shoulders

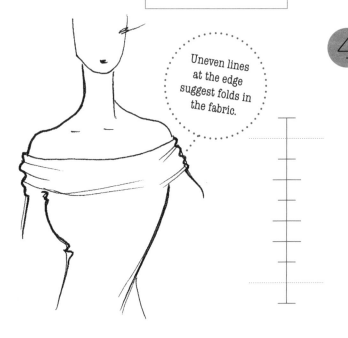

Uneven lines at the edge suggest folds in the fabric.

waist

4

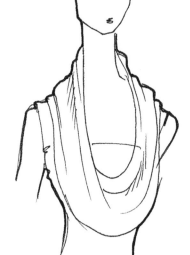

shoulders

waist

Chinese or Mandarin collar

Draw both sides of the stand-up collar, coming together in a small V-shape in the middle of the neck. Draw two lines from the base of the V, for the front opening. Add shoulders, armholes, buttons and loop fastenings.

IDEA

Try a traditional Chinese crossover opening. This runs diagonally across the chest, from the centre of the collar to one armhole.

Peter Pan collar

This collar is named after a Peter Pan costume worn by an actress in the early 20th century. Draw the top edge of one side, to the middle of the neck. Now add the curved bottom edge. Repeat for the other side.

IDEA

This wide, round collar is often used in childrenswear. It also goes well with neat blouses and dresses.

shoulders

waist

A keyhole opening is a nice finishing touch.

waist

Ruffle collar

A ruffle collar adds a feminine flourish to a design. Draw the points where the ruffle will meet the neck, then add the shoulders. Draw two uneven wavy lines for the edges and centre of the ruffle, then add vertical lines for the gathers.

IDEA

Why not combine your ruffle collar with puffed shoulders, or with straight sleeves for contrast?

Drawstring collar

Start with a wide, uneven neckline at the base of the neck. Draw both sides of the drawstring, adding two small circles to show the drawstring openings. Indicate a knot or bead at the tip of each string. Add the shoulders and armholes.

IDEA

The drawstring collar is most often used in sportswear. It is often combined with a hooded top.

shoulders

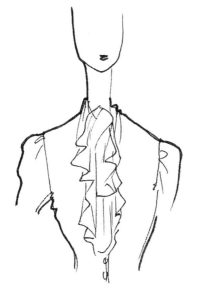

waist

shoulders

waist

Patch pocket

A patch pocket is stitched onto the outside of a garment on three sides. For this pocket, draw the flap, then the front. Draw the side to show the depth of the pocket. Add a fastening in the centre of the flap.

IDEA

Patch pockets are common on clothing worn by soldiers and workmen. Use them if you want a tough, practical look.

Hip or frontier pocket

Draw a curved pocket line at an angle from the waistline to the side seam. Add a small triangle for the inner pocket and top-stitching for detail.

IDEA

This style of pocket is found mainly on jeans. Where else could you feature it?

This style of pocket was designed to hold a watch or coins.

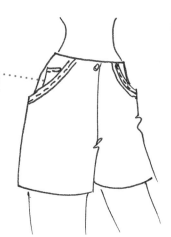

Cargo pocket

On the middle of each leg front, draw a line from the hip to the thigh. This line should follow the shape of the outside hip. Add the bottom and far edge of the pocket. Use top-stitching and add a fastening for detail.

IDEA

Vary your cargo pockets – give them a flap, or combine cargo pockets of different styles and sizes in the same design.

Welt pocket with tab

A welt is a strip of fabric or other material that trims an edge. Draw a long rectangle for the upper part of this welt. Below it, in the middle, add a tab with a button fastening. Add the bottom part of the welt on either side of the tab.

IDEA

Welt pockets are usually found on the chest of jackets and coats. Try designing a pocket with a single welt.

The pocket curves around the outside of the hip.

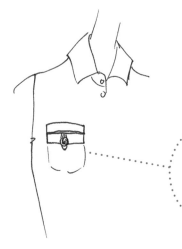

The main pocket lies underneath the outer fabric.

Barrel and French cuff

A barrel cuff is one of the simplest cuff styles. A French, or double, cuff is worn folded back on itself. Holes on both sides allow it to be fastened by pulling the edges together.

Gathered sleeve and embellished French cuff

Some cuffs have decorative details, such as drawstrings or frills. For both these style, draw the sleeves wider as they reach the hands, then curve them in at the cuff.

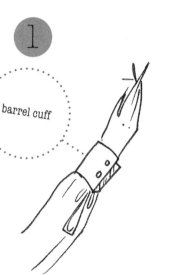

barrel cuff

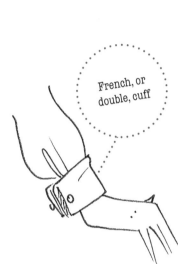

French, or double, cuff

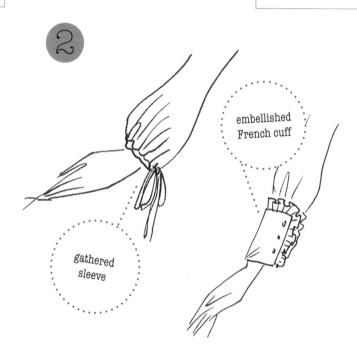

embellished French cuff

gathered sleeve

Frill and zip cuff

Cuffs sometimes extend over the hand. For the frill design, use lines to emphasize how the fabric is pulled together. For a smooth shape, consider a zip fastening to create a tight sleeve.

Ribbed and thumb-hole cuff

Knitted garments often have ribbed cuffs. Ribbing consists of stretchy rows of stitches that can spring back to fit the wrist snugly. In the thumb-hole cuff, the sleeve folds over the hand with a separate hole for the thumb.

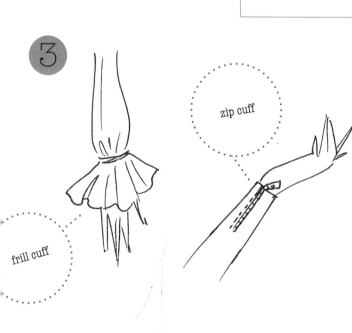

zip cuff

frill cuff

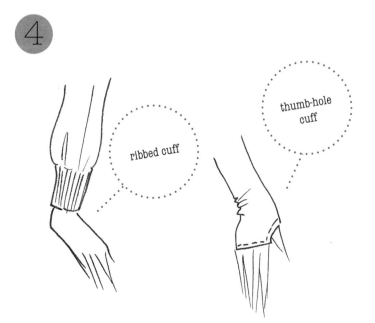

thumb-hole cuff

ribbed cuff

Parts of a shoe

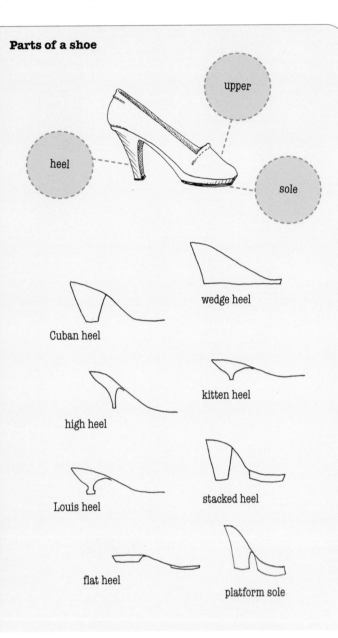

upper

heel

sole

wedge heel

Cuban heel

kitten heel

high heel

Louis heel

stacked heel

flat heel

platform sole

Although shoes and boots come in all sorts of designs, they are all made up of the same basic parts. The drawing above shows the main parts of a shoe – the upper, heel and sole.

There are a number of different heel shapes you can choose when designing shoes and boots. Think about the overall shape of your design and how the different parts balance each other. For example, if you want to use a chunky wedge heel, this would work better with a chunky rounded or square toe. A thin, pointed toe would be best paired with a thin, delicate heel.

Ankle-strap high heel

Start with sole of the shoe – think of it as a platform supporting the foot. Fill in the shoe upper, including an elegant cutaway for the foot. Add ankle straps, button details and shading.

IDEA

Practise drawing feet, ankles and legs before you start designing shoes. Think about the proportions in relation to the rest of the body.

High-heeled sandal

A sandal has straps attached to the sole and can be high-heeled or flat. Start with the side view. Draw the sole, then add the heel and the upper straps. Now draw the other shoe.

IDEA

Look at the foot in side view. See how the line of the sole forms an arch between the flat toe and the heel.

Louis XIV heel

Draw the sole first. Create the upper, with a rounded part at the back. Style the heel so that it curves inwards at the front and back. Add a ruffle detail.

This style is named after King Louis XIV of France, who wore heels like this. Imagine a shoe named after you. How would it look?

 3

D'Orsay mule

The D'Orsay shoe has a cut-out side that exposes the foot. Start with the sole and high heel, then fill in the upper, leaving a gap between toe and heel.

A mule can have a variety of heels, from a chunky block heel, a clog or a curvy spool heel to a pin-thin stiletto or a flat heel.

 4

Loafer pump

There are many varieties of flat-soled shoes, from ballerinas and dolly pumps to slippers. Loafers are practical, casual shoes. Draw the sole with a gentle slope that follows the arch of the foot. Fill in the upper and add a low heel.

In the 1950s, American students started a trend for tucking pennies into the leather uppers of their shoes, and created the term 'penny loafer'.

 5

Open-toed wedge

By raising the foot and filling in the heel, the wedge lengthens the leg silhouette with a flattering effect. Draw the flat sole and wedge. Add the upper with a detailed crossbar and open toe.

Another popular wedge is the high-heeled summer espadrille, made of canvas with a rope sole and ankle ties. What other fabrics could you use?

6

Sculptured wedge

Draw a curved upper sole to support the foot. Then create the shape of the wedge, dropping it straight down from the toe and curving it in and under at the heel. Add straps and shading.

IDEA

Look at pictures of wooden pattens from the Middle Ages. These were worn over normal shoes to raise feet above dirty roads. Look, too, at disco platform shoes from the 1970s.

Rocking-horse shoe

Draw the top sole first. Then draw the large curved platform sole, which rocks the foot as it moves. The original design for this style had leather ribbons crossing the leg like ballet shoes.

IDEA

These shoes were created to go with a fashion collection by Vivienne Westwood. Perhaps you could invent a new style of shoe to accompany your own designs.

The small cut-out at the back of the heel is a key design feature.

Ankle boot stiletto

A stiletto is a thin, sharp heel, named after an Italian word for 'dagger'. Draw the sole at a sharp angle. Place the heel under the ankle, with the upper curving up around the lower leg. Add zips and spurs around the heels.

IDEA

Shoe designer Manolo Blahnik has created a stiletto called the 'needle'. Think of an object to inspire your shoe designs.

Slender, pointed toes go well with the thin stiletto heels.

Open-toed ankle boot

For the side view, use a double line to show the sole. Add a thick, chunky heel that tapers in at the bottom. Draw the upper, curving in over the heel as it rises to the ankle. Add side zips and a cutaway toe.

IDEA

Fashion ideas can be fun rather than practical. Boots normally give feet more protection than shoes — but these have open toes.

Shading describes the darker inside of the boot.

High-top trainer

These shoes were first designed with baseball in mind. They have an upper that covers the ankle. Draw the thick rubber sole first. Draw the upper with a curved heel to show where the ankle is.

IDEA

Think about printing colours or textile designs onto canvas shoes to go with your fashion collection.

These trainers have protective caps around the heel and toe.

Snow boot

Start with a sturdy flat sole, then fill in the heel and back. Add the front with a soft curve around the toe. Draw a short, straight line for the leg opening, and add buttons. Use hatched outlines for the furry tops.

IDEA

Designers love to travel and be inspired by different countries and climates. What country would these boots inspire you to visit?

Slouchy knee boot

Start with the sole. Think about the height of the boots and then draw the legs. Think about the folds in the fabric and the uneven shapes they create. Add shading to highlight the sole and the folds in the fabric.

IDEA

Copy established designers and brands who often include details, such as a logo or coloured sole, to make their designs easily recognizable.

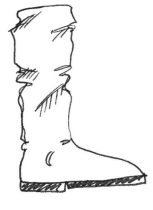

Gladiator sandal

This style became popular in the early 21st century. Draw the sole first. Add the upper, curving it around the heel and ankle to follow the outline of the calf. Add cutaway straps with fastenings around the ankle and over the toes.

IDEA

Images from the past can provide inspiration. This style is similar to the footwear worn by the soldiers you can see in Roman mosaics.

Slouch bag

A slouch or hobo bag has a moon-like shape and shoulder strap. Draw both straps, widening out towards the bottom of the bag. Join these with a soft line at the bottom and a zip detail between the straps.

IDEA

Turn the slouch bag into a clutch bag. Draw a clasp across the top and add gather lines to suggest the fullness of the bag.

Envelope bag

For the top flap of the bag draw a triangle with two equal sides pointing down. Add the sides and base, then the inner triangle. Add a fastening and a strap.

IDEA

Use the same basic rectangle to create the chain-handle bag. Add a gathered band around the middle and a chain strap.

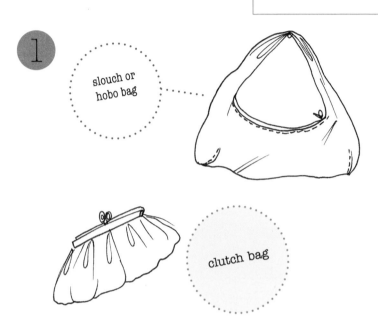

1

slouch or hobo bag

clutch bag

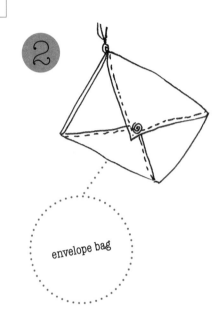

2

envelope bag

chain-handle bag

Structured bag

Draw the bag from the side to show how deep it is, as well as how wide and high. Because you are showing it from the side, the lines are angled. Attach the handle and flap fastening and the studs at the base that protect the leather.

IDEA

Compare the structured bag to the pouch-pocket bag. How are they similar? How are they different?

Braid-handle bag

Imagine the bag as a series of shapes: a central rectangle, triangles at either side, a half-circle for the handle and a long, slim base. Draw the braided, or plaited, handle and add stitching and a knot of leather on the front.

IDEA

Play with sizes – oversized bags add drama to an outfit. How else does the tote bag shown below differ from the braid-handled bag?

3

structured bag

pouch-pocket bag

4

tote bag

braid-handle bag

Cloche and fedora

Compare these two hats. The cloche has a narrow headband, a wide, low brim that rises up above one eye and a round crown. The fedora has a wide headband, a narrower brim that partly hides the face and a creased crown.

IDEA

Practise drawing hat brims that are angled up as well as down, since these show more of the face.

The crown forms the top of a hat.

cloche

fedora

The brim partly hides the face.

Knitted bobble hat and beanie

Start with the basic head shape. Draw a zigzag line around the forehead for the bobble hat. Draw a curved band for the beanie. Join the sides to the crown. Add knitted texture on the bobble hat and crease lines on the beanie.

IDEA

Remember that the tops of both these hats should sit at least half a head above the hairline.

bobble hat

beanie

Try this: adding accessories

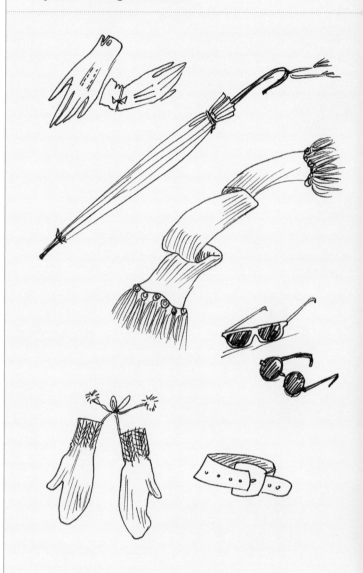

Gloves, scarves, jewellery, sunglasses, umbrellas, belts, stockings, socks and shoes all help to complete an outfit. They are usually sold on their own and not as part of an individual garment because this would then cost too much to make.

Detail is important on accessories, so use a sharp pencil to create a fine line when drawing them. Look carefully at the accessories you wear to see how they are constructed.

Perhaps you can invent a new type of accessory. As technology develops you may want to design accessories for new devices, as well as for computers and phones.

First things first

Before you can start designing, you need to be sure you have mastered your croquis or basic figure. The figure comes first. It is the starting point for your designs. Once you have perfected your figure, you have the tools to start dreaming, thinking and designing.

Fashion designers spend hours drawing, to improve their skills, to get inspiration and to develop their own style. Follow the steps on pages 34–41 again and again, and soon you will be drawing your figure with confidence. Here are some other tips:

Draw regularly
Take inspiration from Zandra Rhodes and try to **do a drawing a day**.

Be patient
It takes time to learn to draw things well, so be patient – and remember that many of the designers interviewed in this book taught themselves how to draw. The British fashion designer Norman Hartnell was ill as a child and spent hundreds of hours drawing in bed. Look back at his interview on pages 20–21.

Keep going
At first, you may feel embarrassed drawing in public, but **don't give up**. Once you have the skills and techniques to draw the figure you can really have fun.

Set aside time
Perhaps you could create regular sessions for drawing. Could you **create your own fashion school** at home and invite friends over to practise?

Develop your own style
How can you **express your own style** with the figure? The model could look like a person you admire, or perhaps like you. Study the drawings of leading designers. The way they each present faces, hair and make-up are key to creating their individual look.

Here are some of the stages you would have to go through as a professional fashion designer. Read more about them on the following pages:

1.

Design brief or concept
You will be given this by your client – the individual person or company that you are working for. The brief is a set of practical guidelines that your designs need to follow.

2.

Doing research
You'll need to do research into fashion trends, and look for information, images and ideas that help you meet your brief. Keep a sketchbook to record your research. Jot your thoughts down there and fill it with rough sketches to explore how your designs might work.

3.

Building a moodboard
A moodboard is a collage that brings together your sketches and ideas. It allows you to see them as a whole, and identify key themes.

4.

Creating a fashion collection
Your collection is a selection of designs that work together as outfits for a particular season.

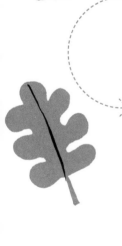

Finding out what's needed

It's fun to design clothes that you want to wear yourself, but usually fashion designers have to work with clients, who have particular demands. As a designer, you will be asked to work to a set of guidelines, which will form the basis of your collection. These guidelines are called a brief.

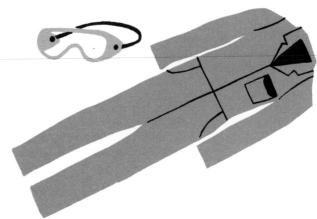

Before you pick up your pencil and get started, you need to find out what the brief is by asking questions about the clothes you're going to design.

Who is the target market? Who will wear your designs?

- **Men** or women?

- Will it be one **person** or a **group**?

- How old are they, roughly? Are they very **young** or **teenagers** or **middle-aged** or **elderly**?

- What's their **lifestyle**? What will they be doing in your clothes? Will they be at work in an office or at a glamorous party?

- What **size** are they?

Which part of the market are you aiming for – high street or couture?

What's couture?
Couture is the creation of exclusive designs by top fashion houses. Usually, the clothes are made from expensive fabrics. Often, the clothes are hand-sewn with lots of attention to detail. Only a few of each style are made. The clothes are shown at fashion shows and set the trend for the season ahead. This is the high end of fashion.

What's high-street fashion?
Often, high-street fashion copies the basic style and look of the couture fashion houses, but the clothes are cheaply made in huge quantities to sell around the world quickly. High-street garments are usually made from cheaper fabric than couture and with less attention to detail. This is the affordable end of fashion.

What's the creative brief?

- Is there a theme that you need to follow or can you go wild and do whatever you like?

Which season? Spring/summer or autumn/winter?

- Think about the types of fabric and colours to suit the season.

- Will your clothes need to be warm or cool?

What's the budget?

- Think about the price range of the clothes. Will they be sold in your local market or at an expensive department store? The answer will make you think about whether to use an expensive fabric, such as silk, or a cheaper fabric, such as cotton jersey.

Five different briefs

Remember, a brief is an important part of the process. It might seem challenging at first, but it can make you think in a focused way. A brief can also provide the creative spark you need to start designing! Now it's time to follow a brief. Which one will you choose?

① NIGHT IN THE CITY

Creative brief
- A high-street chain has asked you to design a collection of party separates with the theme of a night in the city. What do you think your target customer like to wear **out on the town**?

Target market
- **Teenagers** and **young women**
- All sizes
- Popular high-street chain

Season
- Autumn/winter

Fabrics
- Winter weight for warmth, plus lighter weight for layers and glamour.

Budget
- Mid- to affordable price range.

Sample design
- A collection of separates, including two dresses, two pairs of trousers, three tops, jacket or a coat and accessories.

Where will you look for inspiration? Try watching old movies for glamorous ideas.

② FLIP!

Creative brief
- This is a brief for a swimwear range with the theme of surfing and beach life. Think about what you do at the beach and what you like to wear there.

Target market
- **Teenage** boys and girls
- All sizes
- **Independent beach boutique**

Season
- Spring/summer

Fabrics
- Cotton jersey, sports fabrics such as nylon and lycra.

Budget
- Affordable

Sample design
- A complete range of swimwear and beach sportswear for boys and girls, to include cover-ups and jackets for the evening.

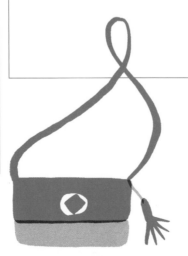

③ TV WARDROBE

Creative brief
- You have been asked to design the costumes for a **new TV comedy** starring a group of young actors. Think about how the clothes can portray different personalities.

Target market
- A cast of **three guys** and **three girls**
- All sizes

Season
- The first episode is set in the autumn with a back-to-school storyline.

Fabrics
- A variety of fabrics to help define the different characters.

Budget
- No budget as these are special costumes.

Sample design
- Design one outfit each for the three guys and three girls.

④

WEDDING BELLES

Creative brief
- In this collection, you will design 'bespoke' (one-off) wedding dresses for individual brides – no other brides will have them. Brides want to be beautiful on their big day so be creative!

Target market
- Bespoke **bridal dresses**

Season
- Spring/summer

Fabrics
- Silks, satins, chiffons, lace and beaded or embroidered fabrics.

Budget
- For a bespoke dress, **prices will be high**. This can influence your design.

Sample design
- Create a collection of **five wedding dresses**. Try a variety of shapes and lengths. Remember, not all wedding dresses have to be long.

Where will you look for inspiration? Old wedding dress designs? Or what might a wedding dress look like in the year 3000?

⑤

The LBD

Creative brief
- The Little Black Dress (LBD) is one of the most popular styles. It's always in fashion. By limiting the colour, you can explore the possibilities of texture and shape. Will the surface be **rough** or **smooth**? Will the dress be **tight** or does it have a **full skirt**? Think surface and shape for your LBD.

Target market
- **Young women**
- **High-street shoppers**
- **Affordable luxury**
- All sizes

Season
- Autumn/winter, especially for the Christmas season.

Fabrics
- Any fabric, as long as it's black!

Budget
- Low- to mid-priced for the high street.

Sample design
- Create a collection of eight to ten LBDs.

Developing your designs

Now that you have your brief, you must find ideas, images, colours, fabrics and patterns to help you develop your designs. Read the brief and start jotting down ideas about where to begin your research.

BACK IN TIME

Books

- Look at illustrated books on **modern fashion** and **fashion history**. It can be fun to take ideas from the past and give them a new twist.
- Visit a **library** to explore the history of fashion more deeply – for example, discover how women first began wearing trousers in the early 20th century, when their lifestyles began to change.

Museums and galleries

- Some of the world's greatest museums were built to record the work of artists and designers. Take a **sketchbook** and draw whatever catches your eye. The smallest detail might be useful.

Who are you designing for?

- Do you have a person in mind when you design? Some designers like to think about a real or imaginary person to inspire them. Perhaps your person could be a **favourite character** from a film, television series or book?

IN THE MEDIA

Magazines and newspapers

Cut out **pictures** and **news stories** that interest you and stick them in your sketchbook. Fashion magazines are a great source but you might find inspiration in **travel** or **science journals** too.

The internet

The internet is a fantastic resource. Find **websites that you like** and, once you have a few ideas, follow them up with further research on the web. **Print out images** you like and stick them in your sketchbook, or save them to your desktop.

ON THE SCREEN

Films

- Visit the cinema and be transported to **different times and places** – it will really get your imagination going.
- Watch a science fiction film to give you ideas for **space-age** costumes.
- Watch an historical drama for **romantic images** of the past.
- Rent films on DVD or Blu-ray and watch them at your leisure – the advantage of doing this is that you can watch again and again to check out those details you liked.

Television

- Watch **fashion makeovers** on television.
- Watch **period dramas** or **documentaries** that feature modern fashions or period costume.

OUT AND ABOUT

Creative brief
- The natural world and the shapes, colours and textures you find there can provide great inspiration.
- The intricate threads of a **spider's web** might suggest a lacy top.
- The colours and textures of **leaves, bark** and **moss** might inspire designs in leather, corduroy and velvet.

Buildings
- Keep an eye out for **interesting architecture**. Curved or spiky, ornate or plain, old or modern, the shapes and surfaces of buildings can all spark ideas for designs.
- Don't be limited to what is around you. Look at **architecture books** for inspiration and sketch or photocopy **pictures of buildings** that interest you.

WHAT'S NEW?

Shops
- From department stores and vintage boutiques to charity retailers and markets, shops of every kind offer a great way to discover what you like and show you what is currently available and popular.

Spotting trends
- Look at the latest **fashion shows** to spot upcoming trends. You can often see pictures of them in newspapers and magazines, or on the television and online.
- What do the new collections have in common? Can you spot **common themes**? Are there similar **shapes** and **fabrics**?

RECORD IT!

Sketchbook
- Try to keep a notebook or sketchbook and **record things** you like when you see them. Go back to these notes for ideas about how you might answer the brief.

Photographs
- Another useful recording device is your **camera**. Carry it with you and photograph anything that inspires you.
- Alternatively, take pictures on your **mobile phone**.

Sorting out your ideas

Once you have a sketchbook full of notes and rough drawings, you can start to collect and sort out your ideas to create a theme. One way to do this is to build a moodboard.

Think about the design brief that you used to do your research. You should have lots of information to choose from. Now you need to sort through what you have found and choose your strongest idea.

What is a moodboard?

A moodboard – sometimes called a storyboard, a presentation board or a concept board – is a kind of **collage**. A 'collage' is a picture made up of lots of different ingredients, all stuck down together on the same background. Your moodboard will be a collage that combines different parts of your research in one big picture. Together, they will make up the **theme of your collection**.

What do you need?

- Find a large piece of A3 card, or use a pin board if you have one. You'll also need glue or drawing pins, and scissors.
- Collect the **images** you have cut out, plus any **swatches** of fabric and any **notes** and **colour samples**. Arrange them side by side.
- Include your **rough drawings** – perhaps you can photocopy these or recreate them rather than tearing them out of your sketchbook.

How do you choose what to include?

- Don't glue anything down immediately. Move the ingredients of your collage around to see if you can spot any connections between them. What do the different parts of your collage have in common? Can you see a **theme** emerging?
- Are there certain **shapes** or **looks** that appear several times?
- What about similar **colours** and **patterns**?

How do you arrange your moodboard?

- When you have discovered your main theme, **leave out** any ingredients that don't belong – the clearer your idea, the easier it will be to start designing.
- Arrange the different parts of your collage in the way that you think looks best. Trim any rough edges with your scissors, then glue or pin the different parts down on the card or pin board.
- Hang up your moodboard or place it where you can see it clearly – and start designing!

What is a collection?

A fashion collection is a selection of garments that work together and that share a common theme. They may all be designed for a particular season, perhaps, or have similar patterns, colours and fabrics.

Have a look at your moodboard and the ideas and themes you see there. Then use these as your starting point for the designs that will make up your collection.

How do you develop your ideas?

- Redraw the designs you chose for your moodboard. A useful trick is to work **across a page** – sometimes with four or more designs in a row. As the drawings progress, you will be able to develop each one from the one before.

How do you choose what to put in your collection?

- Every collection is a balancing act. Deciding what to include and what to leave out needs time, attention and patience.
- Large items such as **coats, jackets** and **dresses** are the main items in any collection. Make sure you include plenty of these.
- **Tops** and **vests** will always be worn with other garments so you can work on these designs later.
- To create a variety of looks and outfits, make sure you balance the number of **tops** – shirts, sweaters and jackets – and **bottoms** – skirts, trousers and shorts in your collection.

How do you know when your collection is ready?

- Professional designers get **feedback** from different people to help them decide when their collections are ready to go into production and be turned into real clothes. Who could you ask for feedback on your collection? Could you invite your friends round for your own **fashion-house show**? They may have some useful ideas that can help you adjust your collection so it's as good as can be!